Salesforce1 Mobile App Developer Guide

Revised Edition

Written by
Dianne Siebold
Samantha Ready
Michelle Chapman-Thurber

With contributions by
Michael Alderete
Cliff Armstrong
Jay Hurst
Dean Moses
Tammy Rahn
Samantha Reynard
Jim Sinai
Quinton Wall
Emily Wilska

Salesforce1 Mobile App Developer Guide

CONTENTS

Chapter 1: Introduction 1

Introducing the Salesforce1 Platform 2
Salesforce1 Platform Features 2
Introducing the Salesforce1 Apps 4
Getting Around in Salesforce1 5
What about the Other Mobile Apps? 9

Chapter 2: About This Book 11

Who Is This Book For? 12
How Do I Begin? 12
About the Sample Scenario 12
About Acme Wireless 12

Chapter 3: Setting Up Your Work Environment 15

Install the Enhanced Warehouse Data Model 16
Download the Salesforce1 App 16

SALESFORCE1 ADMINISTRATION 17

Chapter 4: Configuring Salesforce1 17

Defining Which Users Can Use Salesforce1 18
About Notifications 19
Try It Out: Enable Notifications 20
    Tell Me More: Approval Request Notifications 20
About Offline Access in Salesforce1 21

Chapter 5: Customizing the Salesforce1 Navigation Menu 25

About the Salesforce1 Navigation Menu 26
    Try It Out: Configuring the Salesforce1 Navigation Menu 27
    Test Out the Salesforce1 Navigation Menu 28
How the Salesforce1 Navigation Menu Works 29

Chapter 6: Customizing How Your Data Shows Up in Salesforce1 31

Contents

How Page Layouts Work in Salesforce1 32

    Rethinking Your Page Layouts for Mobile 33

        Try It Out: Create a Custom Page Layout for the Mobile Technicians Profile . . . 35

        Test the Page Layout 36

    Tips for Optimizing Page Layouts for Mobile 38

About Compact Layouts 39

    Try It Out: Create a Compact Layout 40

    Test the Compact Layout 42

        Tell Me More: Compact Layouts 43

Chapter 7: Using Actions in Salesforce1 45

About Actions 46

    Action Categories 47

Point and Click Your Way to Actions 49

    Try It Out: Create an Object-Specific Action 49

        Try It Out: Assign the Action to the Account Page Layout 50

    About Global Actions 51

    Tell Me More: Actions 52

About Action Layouts 52

    Try It Out: Customize an Object-Specific Action Layout 54

    Test Out the Object-Specific Action 55

About Predefined Values in Actions 56

    Try It Out: Set a Predefined Field Value on an Action 57

    Test the Predefined Value 58

About Custom Actions 59

Chapter 8: Guidelines and Best Practices for Administrators 61

Action Guidelines and Best Practices 62

Custom Icon Guidelines and Best Practices 62

DEVELOPING FOR SALESFORCE1 65

Chapter 9: Welcome to Salesforce1 Platform Development 65

Our Scenario 66

Who This Part is For 66

When to Use the Salesforce1 Platform vs. Creating Custom Apps 66

Salesforce1 Platform Development Process 68
Development Prerequisites 69
    Change the System Administrator Page Layout Assignment 69

Chapter 10: Designing Mobile-First User Interfaces 71

Design for Mobile 72
Keep Navigation Simple 72
Put Important Information at the Top 72
Minimize the Number of Fields 73
Use Field Defaults 74
Minimize User Interface Text 74
Tap Target Size 75

Chapter 11: Extending Salesforce1 with Visualforce Pages 77

Try It Out: Create a Visualforce Page 78
    Create a New Tab 81
    Add the Tab to the Navigation Menu 82
    Test Out the Visualforce Page 83
Tell Me More: Where Visualforce Pages Can Appear in Salesforce1 85
Tell Me More: About the Code 87

Chapter 12: Adding Functionality with Visualforce Custom Actions 91

Custom Actions Scenario 92
Try It Out: Create a Visualforce Custom Action 92
    Add the Visualforce Custom Action to the Page Layout 93
    Test Out the Visualforce Custom Action 94
Tell Me More: About the Code 97

Chapter 13: Integrating Your Web Applications in Salesforce1 with Force.com
Canvas 103

About Force.com Canvas 104
Extending Salesforce1 with Canvas Custom Actions 104
    Try It Out: Clone the Shipify Web Application 105
        Create the Shipify Canvas App 106
        Configure Who Can Access the Shipify Canvas App 108
        Configure the Heroku Environment Variables 109

Contents

Add the Action to the Global Publisher Layout 110

Test Out the Canvas Custom Action 111

Tell Me More: Get Context in your Canvas App 114

Extending Salesforce1 with Canvas Apps in the Feed 119

Try It Out: Clone the DeliveryTrakr Web Application 119

Create the DeliveryTrakr Canvas App 121

Configure Who Can Access the DeliveryTrakr Canvas App 123

Configure the Heroku Environment Variables 123

Create a Global Action 125

Add the Action to the Global Publisher Layout 126

Test Out the DeliveryTrakr Canvas App 127

Tell Me More: About the Code to Create Feed Items 133

Chapter 14: Calling Actions from the API 135

Try It Out: Create an Invoice Action 136

Add the Code to Call the Action 137

Test Out Calling the Action from the API 139

Tell Me More: Actions and the REST API 142

Chapter 15: Extending the User Interface with Flexible Pages 153

What is a Flexible Page? 154

About Flexible Pages 154

Flexible Pages: The Big Picture 156

Before We Begin: Download the Deliveries App 157

Creating a Flexible Page 157

Try It Out: Create a Flexible Page 158

Assigning Actions to A Flexible Page 159

Try It Out: Add an Action to Your Flexible Page 160

Deploying a Flexible Page 161

Try It Out: Deploy a Flexible Page 161

About Flexible Page Tabs 162

Try It Out: Create a Flexible Page Tab 162

Tell Me More: Flexible Page Tabs 163

Making Your Flexible Page Available in Salesforce1 164

Try It Out: Add a Flexible Page to the Salesforce1 Navigation Menu 164

Test the Flexible Page in Salesforce1 165

Tell Me More: Flexible Pages 167

Chapter 16: Development Guidelines and Best Practices 169

When to Use the Navigation Menu or the Publisher 170
Visualforce Guidelines and Best Practices 171
 Sharing Visualforce Pages Between Mobile and Desktop 172
 Excluding Visualforce Pages from Mobile or Desktop 173
 Choosing an Architecture for Visualforce Pages in Salesforce1 173
  Standard Visualforce Pages 173
  Mixed Visualforce and HTML 174
  JavaScript Remoting and Static HTML 177
 Visualforce Components to Avoid in Salesforce1 183
  Unsupported Visualforce Components 183
 Choosing an Effective Page Layout 184
 User Input and Interaction 188
 Managing Navigation 191
  Navigation with the sforce.one Object 193
  How sforce.one Handles API Versions 196
 Visual Design Considerations 200
 Using Visualforce Pages as Custom Actions 203
 Creating Visualforce Pages That Work in Mobile and Desktop 204
 Performance Tuning for Visualforce Pages 205
Force.com Canvas Guidelines and Best Practices 205
 Canvas Apps in the Publisher 206
 Canvas Apps in the Feed 208
 Canvas Apps Context 208
 Custom Icons for Canvas Apps 209

Chapter 17: Learning More 211

INDEX 213

CHAPTER 1 Introduction

In this chapter ...

- Introducing the Salesforce1 Platform
- Salesforce1 Platform Features
- Introducing the Salesforce1 Apps
- Getting Around in Salesforce1
- What about the Other Mobile Apps?

Mobile has become the new normal for staying connected in both our personal and professional lives. More and more, we're living our lives connected to the Internet, but instead of sitting at a desk, we're connecting on planes, in cabs, in between meetings, in hotels, or even in line for coffee. We follow friends, update status feeds, research local businesses, collaborate with colleagues, email suppliers, and much more—all tasks increasingly performed on the go.

And at the same time, every company is working harder and faster to innovate and stay ahead of the competition. The successful businesses of the future must embrace this mobile-first world and the freedom this mobility provides to get things done, regardless of where you are and what you're doing.

Salesforce1 solves the problems of lagging innovation and a lack of mobile specialists with a revolutionary approach to app development for the social and mobile-first world. Salesforce1 delivers breakthrough productivity for all users because it puts the customer—employees, partners, consumers, and devices—at the center of everything.

The result is a fast, connected mobile solution with the potential to be as disruptive as Software as a Service. It's time to build the future today!

Introducing the Salesforce1 Platform

Salesforce1 is a mobile app development platform for everyone. It gives ISVs, developers, administrators, and every user the freedom to innovate.

This approach to unlocking mobile app development for organizations is built for today's needs: mobile and social solutions delivered in days or weeks. Apps are driven by metadata and intelligently provide context to the user experience. These apps deliver information-based mobile device features: addresses can be plotted on maps, phone numbers can be dialed with a simple tap, feed-centric workflows can be created, and much more.

Business users and administrators can develop apps with clicks, not code, complete with powerful workflow rules, approval processes, and dynamic user interfaces. Unlike other solutions where business users often create independent applications in which IT has little visibility into their security or reliability, Salesforce1 gives administrators the tools to centrally manage apps without limiting the business's need to innovate.

Designed for scale with open APIs for extensibility and integration, and powerful developer tools, there's no limit to what developers and ISVs can build on the platform. Salesforce1's flexible development models let every administrator or developer create custom apps that are supported by mobile back-end services and a unique, yet familiar, mobile user experience. ISVs developing on the Salesforce1 Platform can develop apps that take advantage of advanced packaging and version management controls, complete enterprise marketplace capabilities with the AppExchange, and feed-first discovery of their apps within the Salesforce1 Platform.

Salesforce1 Platform Features

The Salesforce1 Platform brings together Force.com, Heroku, and ExactTarget Fuel into one incredibly powerful family of social, mobile, and cloud services—all built API first.

The Salesforce1 Platform delivers:

Social Data

The ability to share, follow, collaborate, and take business actions directly on data within Salesforce1 is at the core of the platform. Users can follow records and data with a single tap. They can be notified of changes in real time, and collaborate directly within the record feed. This feed-based approach to working lets users focus on what's most important to them.

By treating data as social and as an important participant in business, Salesforce1 allows data to share updates, trigger workflows, and be part of the collaboration process with workers, teams, partners, and customers. The result is an unparalleled opportunity to create new business apps and processes for business productivity.

Declarative and Programmatic Development

IT departments have struggled to keep pace with the level of change required for businesses to remain competitive. Too often, IT is resource-constrained because they must manage existing on-premises systems while at the same time recruit and retain professional developers—especially those with mobile application development experience.

Salesforce1 solves this problem by providing intuitive drag-and-drop tools for storing and working with data, defining cloud-based logic with workflows, creating approval processes and formulas, and creating mobile-ready apps.

Professional developers can use the most popular open-source languages, tools, and standards to build completely custom apps and user interfaces. Unlike other platforms, Salesforce1 delivers a unique experience where developers and administrators create apps on the same platform, eliminating the effort required to build complicated integration solutions.

Action-Based App Model

Salesforce1 puts the customer at the center of the development process. Rather than require complicated development cycles, apps can be declared through actions: create an order, set a delivery date, select a route, and so on. Administrators can define default values for actions to streamline apps down to the click of a mouse or a swipe of the finger.

Actions defined via the desktop are instantly available in context-sensitive menus on mobile devices. And, for developers building integrations with Salesforce1, actions are automatically enabled with RESTful endpoints capable of accepting either XML or JSON data envelopes.

Connect to Everything with Open APIs

Salesforce provides the flexibility to create apps that connect to everything using efficient and scalable APIs that perform over 1.3 billion transactions a day. Every object or data entity is instantly REST-enabled.

Our APIs include bulk APIs for data loading, social APIs for ubiquitous collaboration anywhere, cutting-edge streaming APIs to support push notification integrations, and metadata APIs that describe every aspect of your app and business such as permissions, data access policies, field types, and user experience.

Introducing the Salesforce1 Apps

The Salesforce1 apps are Salesforce on-the-go! These enterprise-class mobile apps give your users real-time access to the same information that they see in the office, but organized for getting work done in those precious free moments when they're between customer meetings, waiting for a flight...even when they're in line for coffee.

You can get Salesforce1 in different ways:

- As a downloadable app from the App Store and Google Play™. Users can install it directly on Apple® and Android™ mobile devices.
- As a mobile browser app that runs in supported mobile browsers on Android, Apple, BlackBerry, and Windows 8.1 (Beta) mobile devices. This option doesn't require anything to be installed.

Supported Devices

The way users access Salesforce1 depends on whether they are using one of the downloadable apps or the mobile browser app.

You can run the Salesforce1 downloadable apps on these mobile devices.

- Apple mobile devices with iOS 7 or later:
  - iPhone® 4 and later models
  - iPad® 2 and later models (including the iPad mini)
- Android phones with Android 4.2 or later

You can access the Salesforce1 mobile browser app in these environments.

- Apple Safari® browser on iPad® 2 and later models (including the iPad mini) and iPhone® 4 and later models, with iOS 7 or later
- BlackBerry® Browser on BlackBerry Z10 devices with BlackBerry OS 10.2 or later and BlackBerry Z30 devices with BlackBerry OS 10.2.1.3175 or later. (Salesforce1 isn't supported on BlackBerry Q10 devices.)
- Good Access™ secure mobile browser on Android™ mobile devices with Android 4.2 or later and on Apple® mobile devices with iOS 7 or later.
- Google Chrome browser on Android phones and tablets with Android 4.2 or later.
- Beta version: Microsoft® Internet Explorer® 11 browser on Nokia™ Lumia™ 1020 and HTC™ 8X phones with Windows® 8.1. (Salesforce1 isn't supported on mobile phones with Windows 8.0 or on Windows tablets.)

   Note: The Salesforce1 mobile browser app that's available for Windows 8.1 phones is available as a beta version, which is production quality but has known limitations.

In this book, we'll be working with the downloadable apps exclusively, which you can download and install from the App Store or Google Play. See "Enable the Salesforce1 Mobile Browser App" in the Salesforce Help for information on the Salesforce1 mobile browser app.

Getting Around in Salesforce1

Let's take a tour of the Salesforce1 app.

When users log in to Salesforce1, the first thing they see is a landing page. The first item in the Salesforce1 navigation menu becomes a users' landing page by default. If your organization has Chatter enabled, and you haven't customized the Salesforce1 navigation menu to change the first item in the menu to something else, the user's Feed will be their landing page.

The Feed

The Chatter feed shows users their updates, updates to records and people they follow, and updates in groups they follow. Tapping a feed item displays all of the item's details. Pulling down on the feed reveals the search bar as well as the sort and filter options.

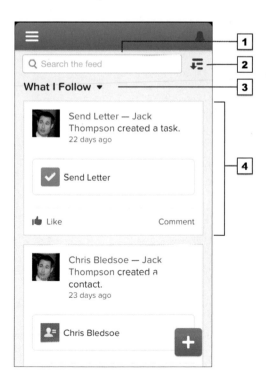

1. Search bar
2. Sort and filter options
3. Feeds drop-down menu
4. Feed item

From the feed, record pages, and from elsewhere in Salesforce1, users tap ➕ to access actions.

The Action Tray

Depending on which feed or record page a user is viewing when they tap ➕, they can see different actions. From the feed, for example, they see a set of global actions. From a record page, however, they see a mix of standard Chatter actions—such as Post and File—and object-specific actions assigned to the layout for that record type. In the action tray, users can tap any action to open it. They can also tap ✖ to return to the page they were viewing.

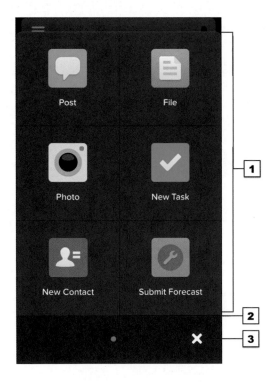

1. Actions

2. Page indicator

3. Cancel

We'll go over creating and customizing actions in Using Actions in Salesforce1 on page 45.

Salesforce1 Navigation Menu

Anywhere users see ☰ in Salesforce1, they can tap it to access the navigation menu.

What your users see in the menu is determined by how you, as the administrator, have configured it, what's available in your organization, and what users have access to, based on their user permissions and profile.

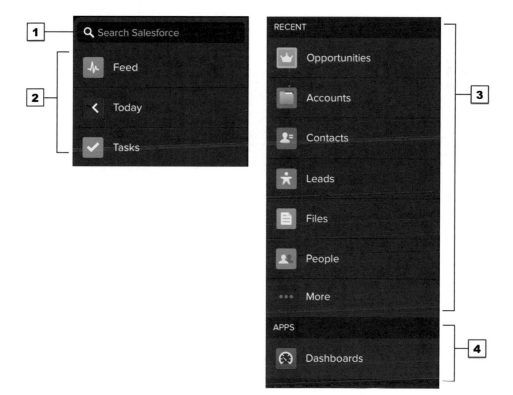

1. Search box

2. Menu items—any items you place above the Smart Search Items element when you customize the navigation menu

3. Smart Search Items—includes a set of recently-searched objects in the Recent section and a larger set of supported objects under the More link

4. Apps section—contains any items you place below the Smart Search Items element

From the navigation menu, users can access the feed, objects, apps, tasks, notes, and any other item you've added to the menu. We'll go over the components of the navigation menu in more detail in About the Salesforce1 Navigation Menu on page 26. But for now, let's take a look at records.

The Record View

The record view is made up of the record feed, detail, and related information pages, which your users can swipe left and right to see. If your organization doesn't have Chatter enabled, the record view only includes the detail and related information pages.

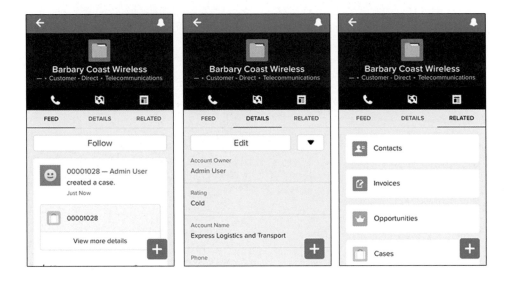

At the top of each record page is the record highlights area. The icon for standard objects is predefined in Salesforce, and you can select the icon for a custom object using the custom object's tab style.

You can customize the fields displayed in the record highlights section by using compact layouts, which we'll look at in About Compact Layouts on page 39.

1. Back arrow—returns the user to the previous page
2. Record highlights
3. Record actions bar—contains a set of predefined *record actions* based on the record's type. These can include Send Email (✉), Log a Call (📞), Map (🗺), View Website (🔗), and Read News (🖼).

What else do I need to know?

From the top of most pages, users can access their notifications by tapping 🔔.

Users can create a new record by tapping **New** at the top of recent object pages, search pages, and related list pages. They can also create and update records by using actions, if create actions have been set up in the organization.

What about the Other Mobile Apps?

Wondering how the Salesforce1 app relates to the other Salesforce mobile products?

- SalesforceA gives administrators mobile access to essential organization management tasks. Use it to edit, unlock, freeze, and deactivate user accounts, reset passwords, and assign permission sets.
- Chatter Mobile for iOS and Android is now Salesforce1.
- Chatter Mobile for BlackBerry and Salesforce Classic for BlackBerry are no longer being supported as of Summer '14. This is because the BlackBerry OS platform on which these apps run is nearing the end of its lifecycle and the new BlackBerry 10 platform doesn't support these apps. Both of these apps will remain fully functional until they are officially deprecated.

Note: Users who have downloaded Chatter Mobile for Blackberry or Salesforce Classic for Blackberry on their devices can continue to use the apps. However, salesforce.com is no longer providing support in the form of bug fixes or enhancements for any issues that your users might encounter. We encourage all customers who use these apps to migrate to the Salesforce1 app on any of its supported devices. Summer '14 includes new BlackBerry support for the Salesforce1 mobile browser app.

- The Salesforce mobile offerings still include Salesforce Classic. Salesforce Classic users might find that Salesforce1 is a better fit for their needs, but Salesforce Classic remains the best option if you need to create and edit in offline mode.

For more detailed information about the full suite of Salesforce mobile apps, see "Salesforce Mobile Products Overview" in the Salesforce Help.

CHAPTER 2 About This Book

In this chapter ...

- Who Is This Book For?
- How Do I Begin?
- About the Sample Scenario
- About Acme Wireless

This book introduces you to both the declarative (point-and-click) and the programmatic (code-based) features of Salesforce1.

To help you get familiar with the different pieces that make up the Salesforce1 Platform, and to show you how you can optimize existing features—such as Visualforce pages and actions—for the Salesforce1 mobile experience, this book walks you through the process of enhancing an existing organization to make it mobile-ready and mobile-friendly.

Who Is This Book For?

This book is broken up into two major sections. The first, Salesforce1 Administration, is aimed at administrators, and takes you through the declarative Salesforce1 tools in Setup, where you can point-and-click your way through getting your organization ready for the Salesforce1 mobile experience. This includes how to optimize your page layouts for mobile, customize the Salesforce1 navigation menu, create actions, and set up mobile notifications.

The second section, Developing for Salesforce1, is for advanced administrators and developers who are comfortable working with code. To fully understand its chapters, you should be familiar with Visualforce, XML, and canvas apps. We'll walk through optimizing your Visualforce pages for mobile, creating custom actions, and creating custom app home pages for Salesforce1 using Flexible Pages.

 Tip: Point-and-click admins, don't let this deter you! We include code samples in most places, so even if you're not an experienced developer, you can still try the steps in each chapter and get a feeling for what can be done with Salesforce1.

How Do I Begin?

It's up to you! You could begin by pointing-and-clicking your way through Configuring Salesforce1 and working all the way through Using Actions in Salesforce1. Then, put your developer hat on and create custom actions, or add canvas apps or Flexible Pages to further enhance your users' Salesforce1 experience.

If you're a seasoned developer, you could jump into the deep end first with the Welcome to Salesforce1 Platform Development chapter.

About the Sample Scenario

The sample scenario for this book builds on the sample Warehouse data and code created in the *Force.com Workbook*. We took that data set and added some extras. We'll use what was built there as a launching point, then add more to bring our sample organization into the mobile world of Salesforce1.

To do this, we'll walk through the steps as if we were someone with administrator privileges at a make-believe company called Acme Wireless.

About Acme Wireless

Let's find out a little bit about our fictional company.

Acme Wireless is a large company that repairs devices such as mobile phones, tablets, and gaming consoles. The company has a number of brick-and-mortar locations where customers can drop off devices for repair. In addition, these storefronts sell device accessories like tablet covers, mobile phone covers, power cords, rechargers, and so on.

Acme Wireless maintains a central warehouse where all the repair parts and accessories are stored. The storefront locations order parts from the warehouse so that they can keep some inventory on hand. When they need a special part that's not in stock, storefronts can special order it from the warehouse.

Acme Wireless is also expanding its repair services by doing on-site service. Mobile technicians will go to various customer locations to provide on-site service, including personal residences, hotels, small business offices, and conference centers.

How Acme Wireless Uses Salesforce

Acme Wireless uses Salesforce to track customers. These are often individuals who visit the storefronts, but can also be small businesses that have contracted with Acme Wireless for device support. Acme Wireless also uses Salesforce to track merchandise items and inventory in the warehouse, as well as to manage its billing and invoicing. They use two custom Web applications: one to track orders and process merchandise for shipment and one to track delivery of shipments to storefront locations.

Employees at Acme Wireless's storefronts and the main office use Chatter internally to communicate about inventory levels, customer accounts, and orders.

How Acme Wireless Wants to Use the Salesforce1 App

Acme Wireless wants to use Salesforce1 to leverage its existing Salesforce organization and enable mobile technicians to access customer and merchandise data. The technicians should be able to see all their repair tickets for the day, locate a customer, look up inventory for any parts needed, order parts, check the status of orders, and so on.

Acme Wireless also wants to enable their truck drivers, delivering products from the warehouses to the storefronts, to track and update their deliveries for the day without having to use a separate app. They also want to give the warehouse workers the ability to track customer orders and process them for shipping.

Acme Wireless also wants to enable Salesforce1 integration with legacy Web applications for order management.

CHAPTER 3   Setting Up Your Work Environment

In this chapter ...

- Install the Enhanced Warehouse Data Model
- Download the Salesforce1 App

To follow along with the exercises in this book, you'll need a Salesforce account and a Developer Edition organization. If you don't have a Developer Edition organization, go to `http://sforce.co/1om1gHf` and sign up for a free Developer Edition account. Developer Edition is a fully-functional version of Salesforce that you can use to develop Salesforce apps. Since it's free, there are limits on the amount of users, bandwidth, and storage you're allowed, but it includes all of the features in Salesforce.

After that, you'll need to install the enhanced Warehouse data model into your organization, and then download the Salesforce1 app, if you haven't already.

Install the Enhanced Warehouse Data Model

To prepare your developer organization for the exercises in this book, you need to import the Warehouse data model. You might be familiar with the Warehouse app if you've gone through the tutorials in the *Force.com Workbook*. We took the Warehouse data from that guide and added a few extra things to it to help show you what Salesforce1 can do.

1. Go to `www.salesforce.com` and log in to Salesforce using your Developer Edition credentials.

2. Open a new browser tab or window, and navigate to
   `https://github.com/forcedotcom/Salesforce1-Dev-Guide-Setup-Package`.
   Do this in the browser that you logged in to your developer organization with.

3. Open the README file.

4. Click the `bit.ly` link in the README file.

   This is the installation link for the enhanced Warehouse data package. You should be taken directly into your development organization to the Package Installation Details page.

5. Click **Continue**.

6. Click **Next**.

7. Click **Next**.

8. Click **Install**.

9. Wait for the installation to finish.

10. From the Force.com app menu, select Warehouse.

11. Click the Data tab.

12. Click **Create Data**.

All right! The last step is to download the Salesforce1 app, then we'll be ready to roll.

Download the Salesforce1 App

If you've already downloaded Salesforce1, you can skip this step.

1. Go to `www.salesforce.com/mobile/`, and download Salesforce1 for your device.
   You may be prompted to create a security PIN.

2. Open Salesforce1.

3. Log in using your developer organization credentials.

CHAPTER 4   Configuring Salesforce1

In this chapter ...

- Defining Which Users Can Use Salesforce1
- About Notifications
- Try It Out: Enable Notifications
- About Offline Access in Salesforce1

Salesforce1 is automatically enabled for all organizations, except those that have auto-enabling turned off.

Salesforce1 doesn't require much configuration at the beginning, but before your users start using Salesforce1, you should:

1. Define which users can access the Salesforce1 mobile apps.

2. Enable notifications.

Since we're in a developer organization, we don't need to worry about enabling users. Review the information about that in the next section, then we'll get started by enabling notifications.

Defining Which Users Can Use Salesforce1

 Important: This information is for reference only. We won't be enabling users in this book, but this step is important when configuring Salesforce1 in your production organization.

Downloadable Apps

The Salesforce1 downloadable apps are connected apps. As a result, you can control the users who have access to the apps, as well as other security policies. By default, all users in your organization can log in to the Salesforce1 downloadable apps.

You can control security and access policies for each of the Salesforce1 downloadable apps using settings components that are installed from the managed Salesforce1 and Chatter Apps connected apps package. These components need to be installed in Salesforce:

- Salesforce1 for Android
- Salesforce1 for iOS

These components are automatically installed when one of your users installs a Salesforce1 downloadable app from the App Store or Google Play on his or her mobile device and authenticates with your organization by logging in to the mobile app.

Alternatively, you can manually install the Salesforce1 and Chatter Apps connected apps package so you can review and modify the default security and access settings before rolling out the Salesforce1 downloadable apps to your users.

When the Salesforce1 connected apps components are installed, they're added to the Connected Apps page at **Setup** > **Manage Apps** > **Connected Apps**. Here, you can view and edit the settings for each of the apps, including controlling user access with profiles, permissions, and IP range restrictions. An error message is displayed if a restricted user attempts to log in to a Salesforce1 downloadable app.

Mobile Browser App

You can control whether or not users can access the Salesforce1 mobile browser app when they log in to Salesforce from a mobile browser. By default, the mobile browser app is turned on for your organization.

1. From Setup, click **Mobile Administration** > **Salesforce1** > **Settings**.
2. Select `Enable the Salesforce1 browser app` to allow all users in your organization to access the app. Deselect this option to turn off access to the app.
3. Click **Save**.

When this option is turned on, users who log in to Salesforce from a supported mobile browser are always automatically directed to the Salesforce1 interface. If you want your users to access the full Salesforce site from mobile browsers instead, deselect this option.

When the mobile browser app is enabled, individual users can turn off the Salesforce1 redirection for themselves in one of these places:

- From the navigation menu in the mobile browser app, by tapping **Full Site**.
- In the full site, by deselecting the `Salesforce1 User` checkbox from either **My Settings** > **Personal** > **Advanced User Details** or **Setup** > **My Personal Information** > **Personal Information**.

Automatic redirection to the Salesforce1 mobile browser app is available in supported mobile browsers only. Logging in from an unsupported mobile browser loads the full Salesforce site.

About Notifications

Notifications let your users know when certain events occur in Salesforce. For example, notifications let users know when they receive approval requests or when someone mentions them in Chatter.

Two types of notifications can appear to Salesforce1 users.

In-app notifications

In-app notifications keep users aware of relevant activity while they're using Salesforce1. By tapping ⬛, a user can view the 20 most recent notifications received within the last 90 days.

If Salesforce Communities is enabled for your organization, users see notifications from all communities they're members of. To help users easily identify which community a notification came from, the community name is listed after the time stamp.

Push notifications

Push notifications are alerts that appear on a mobile device when a user has installed the Salesforce1 downloadable app but isn't using it. These alerts can consist of text, icons, and sounds, depending on the device type. If an administrator enables push notifications for your organization, users can choose individually whether to receive push notifications on their devices.

Some notifications include text that your users enter in Salesforce. To ensure that sensitive information isn't distributed through a third-party service without proper authorization, push notifications include minimal content (such as a user's name) unless you enable full content in push notifications. For example, suppose an in-app notification reads: "Allison Wheeler mentioned you: @John Smith, heads-up! New sales strategy for Acme account." By default, the equivalent push notification would be "Allison Wheeler mentioned you." However, if you enabled full content in push notifications, this push notification would include the same (full) content as the in-app notification.

By enabling the option to include full content in push notifications, you're agreeing on behalf of your company to the terms and conditions displayed when you save the setting. For details, see "Salesforce1 Notifications Overview" in the Salesforce Help.

As the first task in our fresh new development organization, let's set up notifications for all the Acme Wireless mobile users.

Try It Out: Enable Notifications

We want all the Salesforce1 users in the Acme Wireless organization to receive notifications about events happening in the full Salesforce site, such as approval requests, or when they're mentioned.

1. From Setup, click **Salesforce1 Setup** > **Notification Options**.

2. If they're not already selected, select both **Enable in-app notifications** and **Enable push notifications**.

3. Click **Save**.

 Note: Enabling in-app notifications is an all-or-nothing process. Either they're on for everyone, or off for everyone. Mobile users can't customize, enable, or disable in-app notifications for themselves.

Tell Me More: Approval Request Notifications

Users can receive approval requests as notifications in Salesforce1 and can access them by tapping 🔲 or from the Approval Requests item in the navigation menu.

However, some caveats apply to how approval notifications work in Salesforce1.

* If you enable notifications in Salesforce1, keep in mind that approvers may view this list of fields on a mobile device. Select only the fields necessary for users to decide whether to approve or reject records.

* Salesforce1 notifications for approval requests aren't sent to queues. For each approval step involving a queue, we recommend adding individual users as assigned approvers, so at least those individuals can receive the approval request notifications in Salesforce1. To have both queues and individual users as assigned approvers, select `Automatically assign to approver(s)` instead of `Automatically assign to queue` in the approval step.

* Unlike notifications for approval requests in email, notifications for approval requests in Salesforce1 are sent only to users who have access to the record being approved. Assigned approvers who don't have record access can still receive email approval notifications, but they can't complete the approval request until someone grants them record access.

* Individual users can opt in or out of approval request notifications in both email and Salesforce1 via the `Receive Approval Request Emails` user field.

Now that we've addressed notifications, let's look at offline access in Salesforce1.

About Offline Access in Salesforce1

Offline access is available for users in the Salesforce1 downloadable apps only. We won't be working with Salesforce1's offline mode in this book, but this information is important if you have any users who want to take advantage of it.

The Salesforce1 downloadable apps cache users' most recently used records for access offline. Offline access is currently read-only, and is available in the Salesforce1 downloadable apps, versions 6.0 and later.

Offline access is enabled by default when you install one of the Salesforce1 downloadable apps. You can manage this setting in Setup from **Salesforce1 Setup** > **Offline Sync**.

When offline access is enabled, data is downloaded to each user's mobile device based on the objects in the Recent section of the Salesforce1 navigation menu, and on the user's most recently viewed records. Data is encrypted and stored in a secure, persistent cache. This table lists the elements that are available offline.

Salesforce1 Element	Available for Offline Use
Navigation Menu	Yes
Global Search	Previous searches only
Notifications	Previously viewed only
Feeds, Groups, and People	Previously viewed only
Today	Recent Event and Agenda cards on the main view; individual mobile event records available if previously viewed
Salesforce Events	Previously viewed only
Recent Objects	Yes (top five)
Other Objects	No
Record Details	Yes (15 most recent records)
Related Records	Previously viewed only
List Views	No

Salesforce1 Element	Available for Offline Use
Tasks	Only tasks from the first page of the My Tasks list (up to 10 tasks), and only if the list was previously viewed or after the user syncs
Dashboards	Yes (top five)
Approvals (submit, approve, or reject)	No
Visualforce pages	No
Canvas Apps	No
Flexible Pages	No
Settings	Yes

When users switch to Salesforce1, their data is cached, which refreshes the local data store. When a user switches to another app, the user's data is cached automatically if the existing cache is over one hour old.

Users can manually cache their data and refresh that cache at any time (for example, before switching into airplane mode or entering an area with no service), from **Settings** > **Offline Cache** in the Salesforce1 navigation menu.

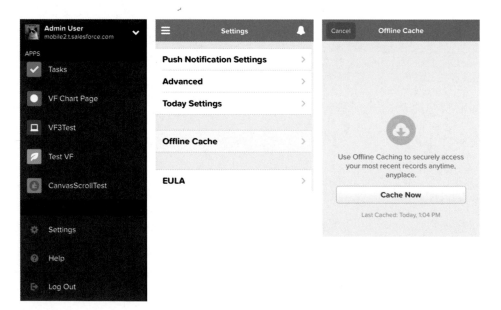

Note: The cache is saved for two weeks. Users can clear the cache by logging out of the Salesforce1 app.

All right! We've addressed notifications and offline access, now let's look at the Salesforce1 navigation menu.

CHAPTER 5   Customizing the Salesforce1 Navigation Menu

In this chapter ...

- About the Salesforce1 Navigation Menu
- How the Salesforce1 Navigation Menu Works

Before you can send your users out on their mobile adventure in Salesforce1, they need a map to point the way to their destination.

The Salesforce1 navigation menu is that map. And it's up to you to draw it for them.

Help your mobile users get work done faster and more easily by configuring which items appear in the navigation menu and in which order.

About the Salesforce1 Navigation Menu

Anywhere your users see the ▤ icon in Salesforce1, they can tap it to access the menu. As an administrator, you can customize what the menu contains.

What You Can Include

Depending on how your organization is configured and what they have access to, your users could see multiple items in their navigation menu.

Menu Item	Description
Approval Requests	Displays a list of the user's pending approvals. Users can tap an approval item and approve or reject it from within Salesforce1. Available in the Salesforce1 mobile browser app only.
Canvas apps	Appears for organizations that have enabled a canvas app to appear in the Salesforce1 navigation menu.
Dashboards	Availability depends on edition and user permissions. If an administrator doesn't include it as a distinct node in the menu, it's automatically included in the set of Smart Search Items.
Events	Lists events that are owned by the user, that the user created for him- or herself, and that the user or a user's groups are invited to. With the exception of multiday events that haven't concluded, past events aren't available.
Feed	Appears for organizations that have Chatter enabled.
Flexible Pages	Custom Salesforce1 app home pages.
Groups	Appears for organizations that have Chatter enabled. If an administrator doesn't include it as a distinct node in the menu, it's automatically included in the set of Smart Search Items.
People	Appears for organizations that have Chatter enabled. If an administrator doesn't include it as a distinct node in the menu, it's automatically included in the set of Smart Search Items.
Smart Search Items	Adds all objects to Salesforce1. This item also adds a set of recently-searched objects to the Recent section and adds the More item so users can access all the objects they have permission to use and that are supported in Salesforce1.

Menu Item	Description
	If you don't include this item in the navigation menu, users can't access any objects in Salesforce1.
	✎ Note: If your users don't yet have a history of recent objects, they initially see a set of default objects in the Recent section. It can take up to 15 days for the objects that users work with regularly in the full Salesforce site to appear in the Recent section. To make objects appear under Recent sooner, users can pin them from the search results screen in the full site.
Tasks	Lists of a user's open and closed tasks and tasks that have been delegated.
Today	An app that helps users plan for and manage their days by integrating their mobile calendar events with associated Salesforce tasks, accounts, and contacts and by enabling users to instantly join conference calls, quickly log notes about events, and more. Available in the Salesforce1 downloadable apps only.
Visualforce page tabs	Only Visualforce pages with the `Available for Salesforce mobile apps` checkbox selected will display in Salesforce1.

We won't get into Visualforce pages in these exercises, but to learn more about them and how they work in Salesforce1, see Extending Salesforce1 with Visualforce Pages on page 77.

Try It Out: Configuring the Salesforce1 Navigation Menu

1. From Setup, click **Mobile Administration** > **Mobile Navigation**.
   Some items are automatically added to the menu.

   The order in which you put the items in the Selected list is the order that they display in the navigation menu. Also, the first item you put in the list becomes your users' Salesforce1 landing page. The Acme Wireless mobile technicians will probably be using the Today and Tasks menu items the most, so we want to put those at the top.

2. Using the **Up** or **Down** arrows, arrange the top items in the Selected list like so:
   - Today
   - Tasks
   - Feed
   - Smart Search Items

- Dashboards

Now whenever a mobile technician logs in to Salesforce1, the Today page will be the first thing they see.

3. Click **Save**.

Let's go look at our changes.

Test Out the Salesforce1 Navigation Menu

1. Open the Salesforce1 app on your mobile device.

2. Tap ☰ to access the navigation menu.

3. Pull down and release the navigation menu to refresh it.
   You should see the Today, Tasks, and Feed items at the top, and then the Recent section, which is created from the Smart Search Items element.

4. Scroll down to the Apps section.

   This section contains any menu item that was put below the Smart Search Items element, whether it's really an "app" or not.

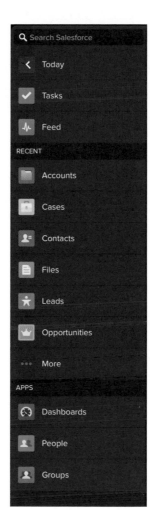

Now that we've addressed the Salesforce1 navigation menu, let's look at configuring our data for mobile.

How the Salesforce1 Navigation Menu Works

- The first item in the Selected list becomes your users' Salesforce1 landing page.
- You can't set different menu configurations for different types of users.
- When organizing the menu items, put the items that users will use most at the top. The Smart Search Items element can expand into a set of eight or more menu items in the mobile experience, and it might end up pushing other elements below the scroll point if you put it near the top of the menu.

Anything you put below the Smart Search Items element will appear in the Apps section of the navigation menu.

- Before you can include Visualforce pages or Flexible Pages in the Salesforce1 navigation menu, you must create tabs for them in Setup at **Create** > **Tabs**.

- Anything that is represented by a tab in Salesforce—such as standard and custom objects, Visualforce pages, the Feed, People, or Groups—is visible for a user in the Salesforce1 menu based on the user's profile settings. For example, if a user is assigned to a profile that has the Groups tab set to Tab Hidden, the user won't see the Groups menu item in Salesforce1, even though an administrator has included it in the menu.

Some objects are excluded from the Recent section, even if you accessed them recently.

- Your tasks and events
- People, groups, and dashboards, if these items were added directly to the navigation menu
- List views, which are shown only on record search pages, not in the navigation menu
- Objects that aren't available in Salesforce1, including custom objects that don't have a tab in the full site

About the Dashboards, People, and Groups Menu Items

If you don't add the Dashboards, People, or Groups menu items to the Selected list for the navigation menu, then they're automatically included in the Smart Search Items set of objects and show up in the Recent section of the menu in Salesforce1. If you do add Dashboards, People, or Groups individually to the Selected list for the navigation menu, then they show up outside of the Recent section and their location in the Salesforce1 menu can be customized, just like Tasks, Today, and other individual menu items.

Pin an Object into the Recent Section

Users can customize the objects that appear in the Recent section of the Salesforce1 navigation menu. If they search for an object in the full Salesforce site, they can hover their mouse over the object name and click 📌 to pin it to the top of the search results. The order of pinned objects in the full site determines the order of the objects that stick to the top of the Recent section of the navigation menu. However, pinning objects in this way causes the unpinned objects remaining in the Recent section to drop into the **More** element.

CHAPTER 6   Customizing How Your Data Shows Up in Salesforce1

In this chapter ...

- How Page Layouts Work in Salesforce1
- About Compact Layouts

We've done the basic configuration for the Salesforce1 app; now it's time to consider how we can optimize things in the full Salesforce site to give our users the best possible mobile experience. First, we'll customize how our Salesforce data shows up when presented in a mobile context.

Two factors in Salesforce affect how information is displayed in Salesforce1. One has been around for a while: page layouts. The other is newer: compact layouts. You'll learn about both in this chapter.

How Page Layouts Work in Salesforce1

You can use the enhanced page layout editor in the full Salesforce site to customize the layout of an object's record detail pages and adjust which fields and related lists appear.

In Salesforce1, page layouts drive these areas of the mobile experience:

Record Related Information and Detail Pages

When you view a record in Salesforce1, you see the fields, Visualforce pages, and related lists that are based on the record type and the user's profile. Related lists show up as single-line cards containing the name of the page or related list. Tapping the related list card displays its details.

Mobile Cards

You can add *expanded lookups*, *components*, canvas apps, and Visualforce pages to the Mobile Cards section of your page layout to have them show up as mobile cards in Salesforce1. The elements you place in this section don't show up on a record's detail page in the full Salesforce site. They only appear on the record's related information page in Salesforce1.

 Note: In organizations that are created after Spring '14, the Twitter component is added by default to the Mobile Cards section of page layouts for objects that support it.

Actions

In Salesforce1, actions you configure on the page layout show up in the action tray when you tap ➕ at the bottom of the object's record pages.

Here are the record detail page, related information page, and action tray for a sample account, Edge Communications:

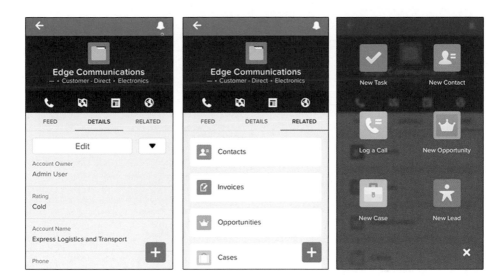

We'll cover actions in a later chapter. For now, let's focus on record pages and mobile cards.

Rethinking Your Page Layouts for Mobile

Page layouts containing dozens of fields and lots of related lists might be manageable when viewing records on a computer screen, but on a small mobile device, viewing that same record can be overwhelming. People accessing information using a mobile device are looking for a quick way to get what they need, and making your users sift through hundreds of fields and related lists just doesn't make sense.

For example, in our Warehouse data model, our custom page layout has 32 standard and custom fields. That may not seem like many, but in a mobile context, fields add up quickly. In the full Salesforce site, an account record detail page using the Warehouse Schema Account Layout looks like this:

In Salesforce1, the same account detail page looks like this:

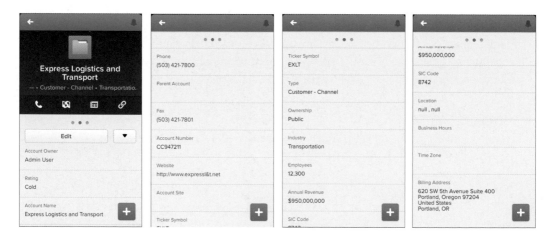

Four pages of scrolling, and that's from a page layout with only 32 fields! If you were a mobile user trying to find specific fields in a record detail with dozens of fields on your phone, you'd have to scroll... and scroll... and scroll. It's not the best user experience, and it's definitely not good for your users' productivity.

You have two options for handling page layouts for your mobile users: re-engineer your existing page layouts, or create new page layouts that are mobile-friendly from the outset.

We'll look at both options. First, we'll walk through creating a fresh mobile-friendly page layout, then we'll discuss tips and tricks for optimizing existing long layouts for a mobile audience.

Try It Out: Create a Custom Page Layout for the Mobile Technicians Profile

Users like the mobile technicians at Acme Wireless will spend the majority of their time accessing Salesforce from a mobile device. We can create a streamlined, mobile-optimized page layout assigned to the Mobile Technician profile, with only the items they need when on-site, and, voilà! Instant productivity boost.

In addition, using the specialized Mobile Cards section of the page layout, we can enhance the Salesforce1 record's related information page by adding Visualforce pages and lookup cards.

1. From Setup, click **Customize** > **Accounts** > **Page Layouts**.

2. Click **New**.

3. Leave the Existing Page Layout drop-down list set to –None–.

   We want to start with a clean slate for this page layout, so we're choosing not to clone an existing page layout.

4. Enter `Account Mobile Technician Layout` in the `Page Layout Name` field.

5. Click **Save**.

   Required fields and "Always on Layout" fields are pre-populated onto the page layout. We just need to add a few more that are pertinent to the mobile technicians.

6. Drag these fields from the palette into the Account Detail portion of the page, below the existing fields.

   - Shipping Address
   - Business Hours
   - Phone

7. Click the Visualforce Pages category in the palette and drag Account Location into the Mobile Cards section.

   This is a preconfigured Visualforce page that shows the user the location of the selected account on a Google map. In Salesforce1, this will show up as a mobile card on the account record related information page.

> 📝 Note: Only Visualforce pages with the `Available for Salesforce mobile apps` checkbox selected will display in Salesforce1. Mobile-enabled Visualforce pages show up as slightly differently colored elements in the palette than their non-mobile-enabled counterparts. Also, hovering your mouse over a Visualforce page element in the palette shows whether the Visualforce page is mobile-enabled.

For more detailed information about using Visualforce in Salesforce1, check out Extending Salesforce1 with Visualforce Pages on page 77.

8. Click the Expanded Lookups category and drag `Parent Account` into the Mobile Cards section.

   `Parent Account` is a lookup field, and putting it into the Mobile Cards section makes it display as a related lookup card on the account's related information page in Salesforce1.

9. Click the Related Lists category and drag the Cases and Contacts related lists to the Related Lists section.

   Related lists show up on the record related information page in Salesforce1. When the mobile technicians navigate to an account's related information page, they'll see preview cards for the related lists that they can tap to get more information about the cases and contacts for that location.

10. Click **Save**.

11. Click **No** when asked if you want to override users' customized related lists.

12. Click **Page Layout Assignment**.

13. Click **Edit Assignment**.

    In this step, you would normally assign the new mobile-optimized page layout to a user profile for the mobile technicians. However, since you're logged in as a system administrator, and we want to show you the changes you're making in Salesforce1, we're going to have you assign it to the System Administrator profile instead.

14. Click the System Administrator line item to select it.

15. Select Account Mobile Technician Layout from the Page Layout to Use drop-down list.
    The System Administrator profile should now be assigned to the Account Mobile Technician Layout.

16. Click **Save**.

Now let's check out what we did in the Salesforce1 app.

Test the Page Layout

1. Open the Salesforce1 app on your mobile device and log in.

2. Tap ▤ to access the navigation menu.

3. In the Recent section, tap **Accounts**. You may have to tap **More...** to find it.

4. Tap the Search bar.

5. Enter *Bar*.

6. Tap **Search**.

7. Tap **Barbary Coast Wireless**.
   You're on the Barbary Coast Wireless record detail page, which is the default view when accessing a record. Scroll down a bit, and you should see the same fields we added to the page layout, in the same order.

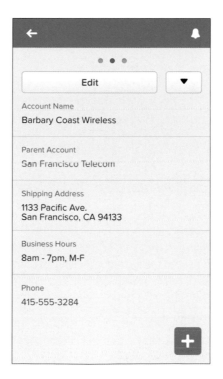

8. Swipe left to the related information page.
   You should see the Parent Account lookup card and the preview card for the Visualforce page first.

Scroll down and you should also see the related lists that we added to the page layout. Tap a related list to see its details.

Now that we've created this specialized page layout and added the fields our mobile technicians will need, their jobs will be much easier when they go on site. When they visit an account record's related information page in Salesforce1, they won't have to shuffle through a long list of unnecessary fields to find the ones they really want. And, since we added the Visualforce page as a mobile card, they'll be able to see the location of an account on a Google map.

In the Actions chapter on page 45, we'll enhance this page layout with special actions we've created just for our mobile technicians. But for now, let's go over some recommendations for paring down existing page layouts to make them more mobile friendly.

Tips for Optimizing Page Layouts for Mobile

In many cases, creating a new mobile-only page layout may not make sense. Here are some tips and tricks to making your existing page layouts more mobile friendly.

When optimizing a page layout, consider:

- What are the important things to see at a glance?

- What are the important moments for your users when they're working in Salesforce1?

- What can you automate so your users don't have to do it?

The Key: Organize and Minimize Fields

- Use sections to organize information logically, putting the most important things at the top of the page so they show up first. Your users don't want to search for fields individually. Organizing similar fields in sections will help your users find what they need. They can then easily scroll down the page to the section they care about.

- For accounts, contacts, and leads, you don't need to put phone or email fields near the top. They're already quickly accessible via the 📞 and ✉ icons on each record page.

- You don't need to keep fields in one column, as the page will render dynamically based on the device that's viewing it. A phone will reorder the fields into a single column, and a tablet or desktop will show two columns.

- Put the most important fields into the compact layout—which drives record highlights and record preview cards in Salesforce1—so they're available right up front, and so your mobile users don't have to drill into the record detail. We'll get into compact layouts in more detail soon.

- Keep the number of required fields to a minimum. Setting a field to required means it must appear on the detail page of all page layouts, so consider whether each field is truly required. You might have to convince stakeholders that a field isn't actually necessary for a record to be saved.

- If available in your organization, think about using record types so that fields that aren't common to all records don't have to appear on all records.

- To reduce the number of fields on a screen, consider using default values for new records instead of having the user enter the data.

We've gone over page layouts. Now let's get into another kind of layout, created especially for mobile: the compact layout.

About Compact Layouts

In the last section, we learned how page layouts affect the look and content of records in the Salesforce1 app. But page layouts aren't the only thing used to help customize how your Salesforce data appears in a mobile environment.

Compact layouts are used in Salesforce1 to display a record's key fields at a glance. Compact layouts are designed for viewing records on touchscreen mobile devices, where space is limited and quick recognition of records is important.

In the full Salesforce site, compact layouts determine which fields appear in the Chatter feed item that appears after a user creates a record with a publisher action.

 Note: To avoid inadvertent sharing of information through the feed, the fields displayed in the Chatter feed items for tasks created using a publisher action are determined by the Task page layout.

In Salesforce1, the first four fields that you assign to a compact layout are displayed in:

- An object's record highlights area
- Expanded lookup cards on a record's related information page

If a mobile user doesn't have access to one of the first four fields that you've assigned to a compact layout, the next field on the layout is used.

The first four fields you assign to your compact layout populate the record highlights section at the top of each record view in Salesforce1, so we'll put the fields we think our mobile technicians most want to see into the list.

Creating and customizing compact layouts for objects isn't required for Salesforce1, because system defaults are provided out of the box. However, if you want to customize which fields show up on object record headers—and elsewhere—for your mobile users, it's a good idea to go ahead and do it. Let's give it a try.

Try It Out: Create a Compact Layout

If you don't create custom compact layouts for an object, all of the object's record highlight fields, preview cards, and action-related feed items are driven by a read-only, predefined system default compact layout that contains a predefined set of fields. After you create one or more custom compact layouts, you can set one as the primary compact layout for the object. The primary compact layout is then used as the default for that object.

We'll create a custom compact layout, and then set it as the primary compact layout for the Merchandise object. Our new compact layout is used to render important merchandise record fields first in Salesforce1 for the Acme Wireless mobile technicians.

Before we can see compact layouts in action, though, we need a Merchandise record in our organization. Let's quickly create one.

1. From the Force.com app menu, select Warehouse.
2. Click the Merchandise tab.
3. Click **New**.
4. For `Merchandise Name`, enter *iPhone 4*.
5. For `Price`, enter *299*.

6. For `Quantity`, enter *1*.

7. Click the `Warehouse` lookup, then select **Oaklandia**.

8. Select Refurbished from the Condition drop-down list.

9. Click **Save**.

Currently, the Merchandise object uses its system default compact layout, which only has the `Merchandise Name` field assigned. Here's what our iPhone 4 record looks like in Salesforce1:

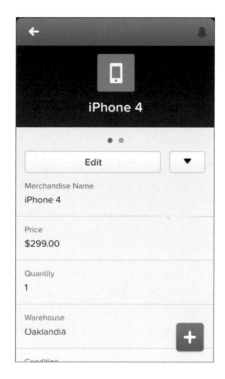

Let's add more fields alongside that "iPhone4" so our mobile users can see more pertinent information right at the top of the Merchandise record pages.

1. In Setup, click **Create** > **Objects**.

   > 💡 Tip: Merchandise is a custom object. If we were creating a custom compact layout for a standard object, the path in Setup would be **Customize** > *Object* > **Compact Layouts**.

2. Click the **Merchandise** object name.

3. Scroll down to the Compact Layouts related list and click **New**.

4. In the `Label` field, enter *Customized Compact Layout*.

5. Select these fields for the compact layout, then click **Add**.

   When on site, these are the most important fields for our mobile technicians to see. You can select and add them individually or select them as a group using CTRL-click.

   - `Condition`
   - `Merchandise Name`
   - `Price`
   - `Quantity`

6. Using the **Up** or **Down** buttons, adjust the list so that the fields are in this order: `Merchandise Name, Quantity, Condition, Price`.

7. Click **Save**.
   Now we need to set our compact layout as the primary.

8. Click **Compact Layout Assignment**.
   You can see that the primary compact layout is set to the System Default here. We need to change that.

9. Click **Edit Assignment**.

10. Select the compact layout we just created to use as the primary compact layout.

11. Click **Save**.

We've customized a compact layout for the Merchandise object. Now let's see what its related information page looks like in Salesforce1.

Test the Compact Layout

When you customize a compact layout and assign it as the default, as we just did, the changes are reflected in Salesforce1 immediately.

1. Open the Salesforce1 app on your mobile device.

2. Tap ▤ to access the navigation menu.

3. In the Recent section, tap **Merchandise**. You may have to tap **More…** to find it.

4. Tap the **iPhone 4** item.

As you can see, the record highlights area has the fields from our newly-created custom compact layout. Instead of seeing just the merchandise name, as on the system default layout, the Acme Wireless mobile technicians can now see much more: that there is one refurbished iPhone 4 in stock at the warehouse, and it costs $299.00.

Tell Me More: Compact Layouts

We've gone over a lot about compact layouts, but here are a few more more tidbits about how they work.

Compact layouts support all field types except:

- text area
- long text area
- rich text area
- multi-select picklist

Users who don't have access to certain fields in Salesforce won't see them on the compact layout.

Removing a field from a page layout doesn't remove it from the object's compact layout. The two layout types are independent.

Compact Layouts and Record Types

If you have record types associated with an object, you can override the primary compact layout assignment and assign specific compact layouts to different record types. If you don't set any record type overrides, all record types use the object's primary compact layout by default.

To find out more about compact layouts and record types, see "Assigning Compact Layouts to Record Types" in the Salesforce Help.

CHAPTER 7   Using Actions in Salesforce1

In this chapter ...

- About Actions
- Point and Click Your Way to Actions
- About Action Layouts
- About Predefined Values in Actions
- About Custom Actions

As an administrator, you can enable valuable micro-moments for all of your users by creating unique actions. When thinking about what actions you might want to create specifically for Salesforce1, ask your users what they wish they could do in the mobile context.

For example, an administrator at a food service company could create an "Emergency Order" action that allows their delivery drivers to immediately order extra or missing food items using their mobile phone while still at a customer site. Creating actions for Salesforce1 can drive adoption in your organization and make you a hero to your users!

In this chapter, we'll learn about types and categories of actions, how to create and customize them in Salesforce using point-and-click tools, and how they can help mobile users get essential work done while away from the office.

About Actions

The publisher actions feature lets you create actions and add them to the Chatter publisher on the home page, on the Chatter tab, in Chatter groups, and on record detail pages. Actions also appear in the action tray in Salesforce1. In addition, actions have their own action layouts, which let you specify which fields are included in the action, and in which order.

In the Salesforce1 app, actions show up in the action tray, which you can get to by tapping .

There are several types of actions you can create using point-and-click tools in Salesforce.

- *Create actions* let users create records. They're different from the Quick Create and Create New features on the Salesforce home page, because create actions respect validation rules and field requiredness, and you can choose each action's fields.
- *Log a call actions* let users record the details of phone calls or other customer interactions. These call logs are saved as completed tasks.
- *Question actions* enable users to ask and search for questions about the records that they're working with.

- *Send email actions*, available only on cases, give users access to a simplified version of the Case Feed Email action on Salesforce1.
- *Update actions* let users make changes to a record from the record's feed.

For create, log-a-call, and custom actions—which we'll go over at the end of this chapter—you can create either object-specific actions or global actions. Update actions must be object-specific.

Object-Specific Actions

Object-specific create actions let users create records that are automatically associated with related records. For example, you might set up an object-specific action on the Account object to allow users to create contacts. If a user creates a contact on the detail page for Acme, Inc., that contact will automatically be associated with Acme. You can only add an object-specific action to page layouts for that object.

Global Actions

Global create actions enable users to create object records, but there's no automatic relationship between the record that's created and any other record. You can add global actions to page layouts for the Home page, the Chatter tab, and any object that supports actions.

Add global Log a Call actions to global layouts to let users record call details from the publisher on the Home page and the Chatter tab. They can also record call details directly from their phone while in Salesforce1.

 Note: Actions to create records for an object that is the detail object in a master-detail relationship must be object-specific, not global.

For a list of supported objects for object-specific and global actions, see "Object-Specific Actions Overview" and "Global Actions Overview" in the Salesforce Help.

Action Categories

Actions fall into several different categories. You may see some but not others, depending on the age and configuration of your organization.

Standard actions

Standard actions are actions that are included automatically when Chatter is enabled: Post, File, Link, Poll, and, in organizations that use work.com, Thanks. Standard actions can also include any you've created for your organization using point-and-click methods, such as create or log-a-call actions.

Default actions

Default actions are create actions—actions that enable users to create records—that are automatically set up to simplify the process of configuring actions.

In organizations created after Winter '14, these actions are automatically added to the default global publisher layout and to the default publisher layout on these objects:

- Account
- Case
- Contact
- Lead
- Opportunity

In organizations created before Winter '14, these actions are available in the palette on the page layout editor for these layouts, but they're not automatically added to any publisher layouts.

Since our Development organization is new, it contains a set of default actions. You can check out the default global actions in Setup at **Create** > **Global Actions** > **Actions**.

For a list of which default actions appear on which object, see "Default Actions Overview" in the Salesforce Help.

Mobile smart actions

Mobile smart actions are a set of preconfigured actions, just like default actions, and are supported on the same list of objects. However, they appear in pre-Winter '14 organizations and are displayed only in Salesforce1.

In Salesforce1, the Mobile Smart Actions element expands to a set of distinct create actions, that enable users to create records directly in the feed.

Mobile smart actions are automatically populated with all of your organization's required fields on the relevant object, regardless of how many fields there are. For example, the New Case action in the mobile smart action bundle includes all required case fields. You can't edit the fields on mobile smart actions; the fields that appear will change only if you change which fields on an object are required.

Mobile smart actions don't appear in the publisher on any page in the full Salesforce site, regardless of which page layouts you add them to; they appear only to users in Salesforce1.

For more information on mobile smart actions, and a list of what the mobile smart action element on each supported object expands to include, see "Mobile Smart Actions Overview" in the Salesforce Help.

Custom actions

Custom actions are Visualforce pages or canvas apps with functionality that you define. For example, you can create a custom action so that users can write comments that are longer than 5,000 characters or create one that integrates a video-conferencing application so that support agents can communicate visually with customers.

We'll touch briefly on custom actions later in About Custom Actions, but you can find out much more about them in the Adding Functionality with Visualforce Custom Actions chapter.

Anchor Actions

Record actions are predefined by salesforce.com and are attached to a limited set of objects. You can't edit or delete record actions.

Point and Click Your Way to Actions

In the next set of tasks, we'll create an object-specific action. But that's only the first step. There are a few things we need to do after that to make sure the action shows up where it's supposed to in both the Salesforce1 app and the full Salesforce site, and that it's optimized for a mobile experience.

These are the steps you need to follow when setting up actions. We'll go through all of them.

1. Create a global or object-specific action.

2. If you created an object-specific action, add it to one or more of that object's page layouts.

3. Customize the action's layout, choosing the fields users see when they use it.

4. Set predefined field values for required fields, where possible.

Let's get started!

Try It Out: Create an Object-Specific Action

Object-specific create actions let users create records that are automatically associated with related records.

Let's give the mobile technicians at Acme Wireless a way to quickly log a case while still on site with a customer. If we put a record create action on the Account object with Case as the target object, the technicians can browse to the customer account record on their mobile device, and log cases directly from there.

1. In Setup, go to **Customize** > **Accounts** > **Buttons, Links, and Actions**.

2. Click **New Action**.

3. For Action Type, select Create a Record.

4. For Target Object, select Case.

5. For `Label`, enter *Create a Case*.

6. Click **Save**.

After saving, we're dropped directly into the action layout editor, where we can customize the fields assigned to the action. We'll get to action layouts shortly. But before we do, there's one more thing we need to do: assign the action to an account page layout.

Try It Out: Assign the Action to the Account Page Layout

Before our object-specific action will show up both in the full Salesforce site and in Salesforce1, we need to add it to a page layout.

1. We're already on the **Buttons, Links, and Actions** node in Setup under **Customize** > **Accounts**. Now click over to **Page Layouts**.

2. Click **Edit** next to Account Mobile Technician Layout.

   This is the layout we created in the Page Layouts chapter. Notice that the Publisher Actions section is empty, and there's a message telling us that any actions on this layout are being inherited from the global publisher layout. But since this page layout is specifically for Acme Wireless mobile technicians, we want to customize the actions on this layout to match the work the technicians need to do.

3. In the Publisher Actions section, click **override the global publisher layout**.
   Default actions appear, and a node for Mobile Smart Actions, which we learned about earlier.

4. Drag the Link, Poll, and Mobile Smart Actions items back to the palette.

5. Click the Actions category in the palette, then drag the following actions into the left side of the Publisher Actions section, in front of Post and File:

   - Create a Case

   - Log a Call

   - New Contact

   - New Opportunity

   - New Task

   In Salesforce1, the first six actions show up on the first page of the actions tray. Since the Create a Case action is important to our mobile technicians, we put it first in the list so it doesn't get lost on the second page of the publisher.

Notice there's also a New Case item in the palette. The New Case item is a global default action associated with the Account object. We're going to customize our object-oriented Create a Case action, so we don't need the redundant global action.

6. Click **Save**.

Our new Create a Case action will now show up in the feed on the Account detail page in the full Salesforce site and in the action tray on account records in Salesforce1 for all of the mobile technicians.

Now that's all done, let's go over global actions. Then we'll revisit action layouts and customize our Create a Case action.

About Global Actions

Global create actions enable users to create object records, but there's no automatic relationship between the record that's created and any other record. Actions tied to specific objects are only accessible from those objects' record pages; however, global actions can be added to any supported objects' page layouts as well as to global layouts, so they're very useful for quickly creating records.

Creating Global Actions

You create global actions in a different place in Setup than you create object-specific actions. To create a global action, in Setup, click **Create** > **Global Actions** > **Actions**. They're called *global actions* because they can be put anywhere actions are supported.

The Global Publisher Layout

Global publisher layouts let you customize actions that appear on Chatter publishers for global pages such as the Home page and the Chatter page. Global publisher layouts also drive the actions that users see when they tap ➕ on the Feed and People pages in Salesforce1. Global publisher layouts can be composed only from global actions. After creating global publisher layouts, you can assign them to different user profiles, which lets you customize which actions the users under different profiles see by default on the global pages.

In Salesforce1, global actions show up in the publisher on pages to which the global publisher layout applies. Before our global action will show up either in the full Salesforce site or in Salesforce1, we need to add it to the global publisher layout.

Tell Me More: Actions

Before you can start working with actions in your own production organization, you need to configure a few settings. We don't need to worry about these in the developer organization we're working in, because they are both already taken care of.

1. Enable actions. You can do this in Setup by clicking **Customize** > **Chatter** > **Settings**, and selecting `Enable Publisher Actions`.

2. Enable feed tracking on any object that you wish to create actions for. You can do this in Setup at **Customize** > **Chatter** > **Feed Tracking**. Select the object, and select `Enable Feed Tracking`.

Action Considerations

- If you add an action to a page layout, but a user assigned to the profile that uses that page layout can't see the action either in the full Salesforce site or in Salesforce1, it might be because:
  - If it's a create action, the profile might not have access to create the record type of the action.
  - The user doesn't have both Read and Edit permission on the action's relationship field. The relationship field is the field that's automatically populated on the target object when a user creates a record using an action. For example, for an action on case that lets users create child cases, the default relationship field is `Parent Case`. To be sure users can see the Create Child Case action, check that they have both Read and Edit permission on the `Parent Case` field.

- You can remove a required field from the action layout, but make sure that the field has a predefined value. Otherwise, users won't be able to create records.

  💡 **Tip:** Did you know that you can drag the publisher icon (➕) into either the lower left or lower right corner of the Salesforce1 screen? Try it!

For more tips, see Action Guidelines and Best Practices on page 62.

About Action Layouts

Just as object record pages have page layouts that can be customized, actions have action layouts that can be customized. We do this in the action layout editor.

When you create an action, its layout is populated with a default set of fields. Use the action layout editor to specify which fields to include in the layout. You can add and remove fields, or simply reorder them on the layout.

The action layout editor has a palette on the upper section of the screen, and the action layout is below it. The palette contains fields from the action's target object that you can add to the action layout. However, the following field types aren't supported and won't show up in the palette:

- Record type fields
- Read-only field types such as roll-up summary, formula, and auto-number fields
- Read-only system fields such as `Created By` or `Last Modified By`

 📝 Note: If you convert a field's type from one that is supported for actions to a type that isn't supported, the field is removed from the action layout. If you convert the field back to a supported type without changing the action layout, the field is automatically added back onto the layout. If you've edited the layout and then convert the field back to a supported type, you must add the field back onto the layout manually.

Try It Out: Customize an Object-Specific Action Layout

The first time you view the layout for an action you've created, certain fields are prepopulated: target object default fields, standard required fields, and any custom universally-required fields. We're going to add more fields to the Create a Case action so the mobile technicians can put more information into the case for the Acme Wireless support reps.

1. In Setup, go to **Customize** > **Accounts** > **Buttons, Links, and Actions**.

2. Click **Layout** next to our Create a Case action.

    The action has four fields already set by default: `Contact Name`, `Status`, `Subject`, and `Description`. The red asterisk next to the `Status` field shows that it's a required field. Let's add a few more fields.

3. Click and drag `Priority` into position right after `Status`.

4. Click and drag `Product` into position right after `Priority`.

    This field lets the technicians indicate what product the customer is having trouble with.

Contact Name
Sample Contact

Status *
Sample Status

Priority
Sample Priority

Product
Sample Product

Subject
Sample Subject

Description
Sample Description

5. Click **Save**.

Now when the Acme Wireless mobile technicians view an account in Salesforce1, they can create a case from any account record page. Let's give it a try.

Test Out the Object-Specific Action

When you create an action, assign it to a page layout, and customize its action layout, as we did, the changes are reflected in Salesforce1 immediately.

1. Open the Salesforce1 app on your mobile device.

2. Tap ☰ to access the navigation menu.

3. In the Recent section, tap **Accounts**.

4. Tap **Barbary Coast Wireless**.

5. Tap ➕.
   Our Create a Case action is the first action in the publisher.

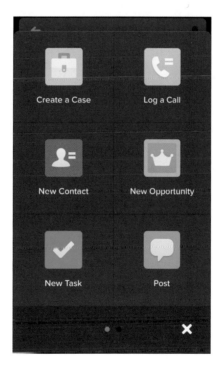

6. Tap the Create a Case action.

7. Tap the Contact Name field.

8. Tap **Lloyd Benjamin** to assign him to the case.

9. Leave its status as New.

10. Assign the case a low priority.

11. Tap **Product**, and select the first one on the list.

12. Enter a subject and description.

13. Tap **Submit**.

OK, we're back on the account record detail page. Swipe right to get to the feed page, and you should see a new feed item for the case you just created.

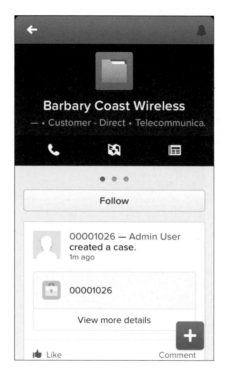

Nice work!

About Predefined Values in Actions

Setting up *predefined values* for certain fields on actions can increase your mobile users' productivity and optimize the action for the mobile environment at the same time.

When configuring action layouts, having fewer fields is better. If you remove required fields from an action layout, the action won't save properly when a user tries it. You have to balance ease of use with the need for required information. Some objects might have many required fields, and when a user clicks a record create action for these, the action layout can be long and filled with required fields. Most users, especially mobile users, don't want to take the time to fill in a whole lot of required fields. They want to get things done and move on to their next task.

If you predefine values for fields on object records created through an action, you don't need to add those fields to the action layout. For example, on an action that lets users create opportunities, you might set Prospecting as the predefined value for the `Stage` field. All new opportunities created through that action will automatically be assigned to the prospecting stage.

You can set predefined values for any field available in the action layout editor, with these exceptions.

- Rich text area fields
- Multi-select picklists
- Read-only field types like auto-number, formula, and roll-up summary fields

Predefined values for fields on actions are separate from default values that you can set for fields on records. A field, if it's included in an action, can have both a predefined value set for when it's used in an action *and* a default value set. If a field on an action has both a predefined value and a default value set, the action uses the predefined value, not the default value.

Let's set a predefined value for one of the fields on our Create a Case action.

Try It Out: Set a Predefined Field Value on an Action

When we customized our Create a Case action, the `Status` field was already present, because it's a required field for cases. Whenever Acme Wireless' mobile technicians are out in the field and have to open a case, the case status is always going to be "New" for them. Rather than require them to fill in the `Status` field every time they open a case, let's set up a predefined field value for it as "New". Then we can remove it from the action layout, and whenever the Create a Case action is used to create a case, the status will automatically be set to "New".

1. In Setup, go to **Customize** > **Accounts** > **Buttons, Links, and Actions**.
2. Click **Create a Case**.
3. In the Predefined Values related list, click **New**.
4. From the Field Name drop-down list, select Status.
5. Set its value to New.
6. Click **Save**.
   Now we need to remove the `Status` field from the action layout
7. On the action detail page, click **Edit Layout**.
8. Click the `Status` field on the layout and drag it up to the palette.

> 💡 **Tip:** You can remove a required field from the action layout, but make sure that the field has a predefined value. Otherwise, users won't be able to create records.

9. Click **Save**.

👁 **Example:** OK, now let's see it in action.

Test the Predefined Value

1. Open the Salesforce1 app on your mobile device.

2. Tap ☰ to access the navigation menu.

3. In the Recent section, tap **Accounts**. You may have to tap **More...** to find it.

4. Tap **Barbary Coast Wireless**.

5. Tap ➕.

6. Tap the **Create a Case** action.
   Notice the `Status` field is now gone.

7. Assign the case a High priority.

8. Tap **Product**, and select any of the products on the list.

9. Enter a subject and description.

10. Tap **Submit**.
    Swipe right to get to the feed page, and you should see a new feed item for the case you just created.

11. Tap the case number in the feed item.
    In the record highlights area of the case record page, you'll see the subject, priority (High), status (New), and the case number. The `Status` field was populated for us, thanks to our predefined value.

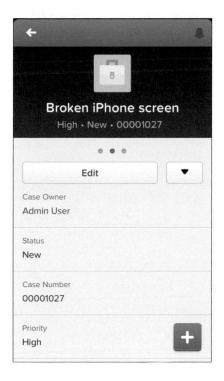

All right! We're almost done with actions. There's one more type, custom actions, that we'll go over briefly for now.

About Custom Actions

Object-specific custom actions are Visualforce pages or canvas apps that let users interact with or create records that have a relationship to an object record. The Visualforce page for an object-specific custom action must include the standard controller for the relevant object. For example, to create a custom action that lets users import a contact's Twitter profile and add that information to a contact record, you need to use the standard contact controller.

Use a Visualforce page or a canvas app to create a global custom action for tasks that don't require users to interact with or create records that have a relationship to a specific object. Canvas apps that you want to use as custom actions need to use Publisher as a location. Visualforce pages that you want to use as global custom actions can't use standard controllers. For example, if you want to create a custom action that lets users enter a street address and see a map, the local time, and the local weather, create a Visualforce page that doesn't use any of the standard controllers, and add it as a custom global action.

We can't create custom actions with point-and-click, so we won't be working with them in our administrator exercises. If you want to find out more about custom actions, see Adding Functionality with Visualforce Custom Actions on page 91.

CHAPTER 8 Guidelines and Best Practices for Administrators

In this chapter ...

- Action Guidelines and Best Practices
- Custom Icon Guidelines and Best Practices

We've covered the primary places you can use point-and-click tools to optimize your organization for Salesforce1 and your mobile users. We enabled notifications, created page layouts and compact layouts, set up publisher actions, and customized the Salesforce1 navigation menu.

In this chapter, we'll cover some suggestions and best practices for actions and custom icons that can make your mobile users' experience that much better. And in case you missed it, don't forget to review the page layout guidelines in Tips for Optimizing Page Layouts for Mobile on page 38.

Action Guidelines and Best Practices

Actions are a great way to let your users get work done quickly. As an administrator, you're in a prime position to give them the exact actions that they need.

When considering what kinds of actions to create, or even when creating the actions themselves, keep these suggestions in mind.

- When customizing action layouts, consider what your users will do with them. Minimalism is key. Include only the fields that are necessary for them and for whomever will handle the cases, calls, or records that result from those actions.

- Don't use actions for simple navigation shortcuts. They're designed to perform a function.

- Give your actions task-oriented names that tell your users what they do. Use terms such as New, Create, Share, Update, or Import. Keep the names short and descriptive.

- Create a global action if you're contemplating something that your users need to do that isn't tied to a specific object and that you want to be accessible from anywhere.

- Use the `Description` field to create notes for yourself about each action. This is especially useful if you're creating several similar actions for different record types, for example. The description appears in the list of buttons, links, and actions for object-specific actions, or in the list of global actions, as well as on the detail page for the action. Your notes aren't visible to users.

- There is no hard limit to the number of fields you can add to an action layout. However, for optimum usability, we recommend a maximum of 8 fields. Adding more than 20 fields can severely impact user efficiency. To reduce the number of fields in your layout, you can create predefined values for the required fields, and then remove those fields from your layout. You can set predefined field values from the action detail page.

Custom Icon Guidelines and Best Practices

You can add custom icons to your actions or custom tabs if your organization has access to the Documents tab.

If you decide to create your own action or tab icon, upload it to a Documents folder and make sure `Externally Available Image` is selected.

When creating a custom icon, follow these image guidelines. The icon should:

- Be less than 10k in size
- Be 120 x 120 pixels
- Be a PNG with a transparent background

- Have a resolution of 72 dpi
- Not include a color background
- Not include outer shadows on the inner icon graphic

In addition, follow these visual guidelines.

- Center inner icon graphics within a 80 x 80 pixel area, leaving 20 pixels of spacing surrounding it in a 120 x 120 px final format.
- The icon graphic should be white, or lighter than the background color.
- Avoid heavy inner or outer shadows.
- Use simple and flat styling resembling the Salesforce1 icon family. See the *Salesforce1 Style Guide* for examples.

You assign custom icons using the **Change Icon** link when you create the action or tab.

You can also customize the icon that is used in the navigation menu for canvas apps. See Custom Icons for Canvas Apps on page 209.

DEVELOPING FOR SALESFORCE1

CHAPTER 9   Welcome to Salesforce1 Platform Development

In this chapter ...

- Our Scenario
- Who This Part is For
- When to Use the Salesforce1 Platform vs. Creating Custom Apps
- Salesforce1 Platform Development Process
- Development Prerequisites

Welcome to development for the Salesforce1 Platform. In Part I, Salesforce1 Administration, you learned how to set up and configure your organization for Salesforce1. You also learned how to customize the Salesforce1 app for mobile users by using declarative programming features. In this part, you'll learn how you can use the Salesforce1 Platform features to extend the Salesforce1 app and add new functionality for your users with code.

Developing for mobile users in Salesforce1 means you can leverage your existing skills to extend and customize the app for your users. You can use the Salesforce1 Platform to extend your organization and then make those changes available to both mobile users and users of the full Salesforce site.

Our Scenario

We'll continue the business scenario of Acme Wireless and build functionality to meet the needs of their mobile technicians and warehouse workers.

You'll learn how to:

- Optimize the mobile experience for users by employing mobile-first user interface design.
- Implement Visualforce pages so that mobile users can access them from the navigation menu, from a record, or from the publisher.
- Create a Visualforce custom action to make a Visualforce page available from the publisher.
- Create a canvas custom action to make a Force.com Canvas app available from the publisher.
- Give users access to functionality in the feed and embed a canvas app in the Chatter feed.
- Leverage existing logic in custom actions by calling them from the API.
- Extend the user interface by creating Flexible Pages.
- Implement development best practices when extending Salesforce1.

Who This Part is For

Part II of this book is geared towards all developers who need to customize the Salesforce1 app with code, from beginner to seasoned pro.

If you're familiar with programming in the Force.com platform or have done development using the Mobile SDK, then you should be able to easily make the jump to developing in the Salesforce1 Platform.

If you're new to the platform or have done mostly declarative programming, then don't worry. Each chapter takes you step-by-step through the process of implementing each feature for our fictitious business, Acme Wireless. This way, you can learn by doing. These sections are titled "Try It Out."

In each chapter you'll also find information about what the feature is, how it works, and when to use it. These sections are titled "Tell Me More." Go there to delve into the details of the feature.

When to Use the Salesforce1 Platform vs. Creating Custom Apps

When it comes to developing functionality for your Salesforce mobile users, you have options. Here are some differences between extending the Salesforce1 app and creating custom apps using the Mobile SDK or other tools.

Salesforce1 Platform

- Has a defined user interface.
- Has full access to Salesforce data.
- Can be used to create an integrated experience in the Salesforce1 app.
- Gives you a way to include your own apps/functionality with publisher actions.
- Lets you customize Salesforce1 with point-and-click or programmatic customizations.
- Lets you add functionality programmatically through Visualforce pages or Force.com Canvas apps.
- Has defined navigation points. Salesforce1 customizations or apps adhere to the Salesforce1 navigation. So, for example, a Visualforce page can be called from the navigation menu or from the publisher.
- Enables you to leverage existing Salesforce development experience, both point-and-click and programmatic.
- Is included in all Salesforce editions and supported by salesforce.com.

Custom Apps

Custom apps can be either free-standing apps you create with Salesforce Mobile SDK or browser apps using plain HTML5 and JQueryMobile/Ajax. With custom apps, you can:

- Define a custom user experience.
- Access Salesforce data using REST APIs in native and hybrid local apps, or with Visualforce in hybrid apps using JavaScript Remoting. In HTML5 apps, do the same using JQueryMobile and Ajax.
- Brand your user interface for customer-facing exposure.
- Create standalone mobile apps, either with native APIs using Java for Android or Objective C for iOS, or through a hybrid container using JavaScript and HTML5 (Mobile SDK only).
- Distribute apps through mobile industry channels, such as the Apple App Store or Google Play (Mobile SDK only).
- Configure and control complex offline behavior (Mobile SDK only).
- Use push notifications (available for Mobile SDK native apps only).
- Design a custom security container using your own OAuth module (Mobile SDK only).

Other important Mobile SDK considerations:

- Open-source SDK, downloadable for free through npm installers as well as from GitHub. No licensing required.
- Requires you to develop and compile your apps in an external development environment (Xcode for iOS, Eclipse or similar for Android).

- Development costs range from $0 to $1M or more, plus maintenance costs.

Salesforce1 Platform Development Process

The Salesforce1 app is designed to run on a mobile device, like a phone or tablet, but that doesn't mean you have to develop on one. Especially when you're working with Visualforce pages that will apper in both the Salesforce1 app and the full Salesforce site, it's convenient to develop on your desktop. By accessing the Salesforce1 app in a device emulator or browser window, you can develop iteratively on your desktop, without having to pick up your device to test each change.

🛇 **Important:** Running the Salesforce1 app in an emulator or desktop browser isn't supported for normal use, and it's not a substitute for full testing of your custom apps and pages on your organization's supported mobile devices.

To view your Salesforce1 custom pages and apps on a device emulator, download and install the appropriate SDK for your supported devices.

- Apple iOS Simulator for iPhone and iPad

  ```
  developer.apple.com/library/ios/documentation/IDEs/
  Conceptual/iOS_Simulator_Guide/
  ```

- Android Virtual Device Emulator for Phone and Tablet

  ```
  developer.android.com/tools/devices/emulator.html
  ```

To view your Salesforce1 custom pages and apps in your desktop browser, access the URL `https://<Salesforce_instance>/one/one.app`.

- For development purposes only, the following desktop browsers are recommended:
  - Chrome on Windows
  - Chrome or Safari on Mac OS X

- To avoid an automatic redirect back to the standard version of Salesforce, set your browser's user agent to that of a mobile device, such as an iPhone or iPad. You can set the user agent in your browser settings, and the steps vary depending on the browser. For more information, see `http://osxdaily.com/2013/01/16/change-user-agent-chrome-safari-firefox/`.

You can't use the standard `https://<Salesforce_instance>/apex/yourPageName` URL to test Visualforce in Salesforce1. You can only do that by accessing the page within Salesforce1.

Development Prerequisites

You'll need to have these before you can start these exercises.

- Access to a Developer Edition organization.

  If you aren't already a member of the Force.com developer community, go to `http://sforce.co/1om1gHf` and follow the instructions for signing up for a Developer Edition organization. Even if you already have Enterprise Edition, Unlimited Edition, or Performance Edition, use Developer Edition for developing, staging, and testing your solutions against sample data to protect your organization's live data.

- The "API Enabled" permission must be enabled for your Developer Edition organization. This permission is enabled by default, but might have been changed by an administrator.

- The Warehouse data model must be installed in your Developer Edition organization and the Salesforce1 app installed on a mobile device. If you haven't already set up these items, see Setting Up Your Work Environment on page 15.

Change the System Administrator Page Layout Assignment

We've created a custom page layout to help us illustrate some of the concepts in this book. Before we begin, let's switch the page layout assignment for our System Administrator profile to this new layout.

1. In Setup, click **Manage Users** > **Profiles**.
2. Select the System Administrator profile.
3. In the Page Layouts section, find Account, and click **View Assignment**.
4. Click **Edit Assignment**.
5. Click the System Administrator line item.
6. Select Warehouse Schema Account Layout from the Page Layout to Use drop-down list.
7. Click **Save**.

All right! Now we're ready to roll.

CHAPTER 10 Designing Mobile-First User Interfaces

In this chapter ...

- Design for Mobile
- Keep Navigation Simple
- Put Important Information at the Top
- Minimize the Number of Fields
- Use Field Defaults
- Minimize User Interface Text
- Tap Target Size

In this chapter, we'll learn about user interface design considerations to keep in mind when developing functionality for Salesforce1 mobile users.

Designing your user interface with mobile in mind is critical to the success of your app. If users find your functionality easy to use and in alignment with the experience they have with other mobile apps, they'll be much happier with the app. The user interface guidelines in this chapter address key differences in the mobile platform and the way users work in it:

- Mobile devices have smaller screens.
- Navigation is done with gestures like tapping and swiping.
- Users typically perform focused tasks from mobile devices like adding a new record.

Throughout the examples in this book, we demonstrate these best practices. As you develop and create your own customizations and apps using the Salesforce1 Platform, keep these guidelines in mind.

Design for Mobile

When designing a user interface for Salesforce1 users, keep the smaller form factor and the way users work in mind from the start.

In the mobile paradigm, users work in quick bursts, spending not more than a minute or two on a task. So be sure to design your app for the way users work.

Avoid taking forms and workflow designed for the desktop environment and simply making them available in Salesforce1. For example, it may be an acceptable user experience in a desktop Web browser to have a form with many fields and related lists on it. However, that same form probably won't provide a good user experience when used from a mobile device.

Users will have a much better experience with forms that follow these user interface guidelines and are designed specifically for the mobile environment.

Keep Navigation Simple

Design your customizations so that users can get to the screen quickly and know where they are within the app.

When creating forms, be sure that they have a simple, logical flow. This helps users to know where they are and keeps them from having to remember where they came from. For example, avoid creating a feed item that links to another form that then links to another form.

Put Important Information at the Top

Put the most essential information at the top of the screen so that it's immediately visible to the user and easy to access.

For example, on a screen that the mobile technician uses to see all their repair appointments, put the most important customer data such as name, address, and phone number at the top. For each screen, identify what the user's task is and what data they need to accomplish that task. Another example is if you're generating feed items, the text should be as concise as possible and the most important information should be at the beginning of the post, as shown in the following example.

Minimize the Number of Fields

When it comes to presenting fields on a screen, less is more. Give users only the fields they need to complete the task at hand.

For example, if you're creating a screen for adding a new warehouse, you might only want to surface the warehouse name field. This way the user can quickly add a new warehouse. If the user has collected more information, they can edit the new record and add it in the detail view.

This guideline is particularly important when displaying information that's for viewing only. For example, if you're creating a form that the mobile technician uses to look up a customer, the technician probably needs to see only the customer name, address, and a phone number. In our page to search for merchandise, only two fields are needed: the merchandise name and delivery distance.

Screen controls should be large enough for users to tap easily and take into account that every user's hands are sized differently. Controls that are too small means users will need to tap multiple times, a frustrating experience. But you don't want controls so large that users can accidentally tap one when they meant to tap another.

We recommend a minimum tap target size of 44 pixels wide by 44 pixels high. For more information about custom icons, see Custom Icon Guidelines and Best Practices on page 62.

CHAPTER 11   Extending Salesforce1 with Visualforce Pages

In this chapter ...

- Try It Out: Create a Visualforce Page
- Tell Me More: Where Visualforce Pages Can Appear in Salesforce1
- Tell Me More: About the Code

You can use your knowledge of Visualforce to extend the Salesforce1 app and give your mobile users the functionality they need.

In this chapter, we'll extend the Acme Wireless organization and give mobile technicians a way to find nearby warehouses. For example, if the technician is out on a call and needs a part, they can use this page to look for warehouses within a 20–mile radius.

While you could take an existing Visualforce page and surface it in Salesforce1, you should consider how that page will look and function on a mobile device. Most likely, you'll want to create a new page designed especially for a mobile experience.

For more information about where Visualforce pages can appear in the user interface, see Tell Me More: Where Visualforce Pages Can Appear in Salesforce1 on page 85.

Now, let's get started!

Try It Out: Create a Visualforce Page

Now we'll create a Visualforce page and make it available from the navigation menu.

This Visualforce page references these items.

- A static resource named `googleMapsAPI`
- An Apex class named `FindNearby`

These have been provided for you in the package that you downloaded and installed for this guide.

Also included in the package is the Visualforce page `FindNearbyWarehousesPage`. You can move on to the next step, Create a New Tab on page 81, if you want to use the page included in the package.

The code for this page uses the location of the current user and integrates with Google Maps to display a map with warehouses located within 20 miles. For each nearby warehouse, the map displays a pin along with the warehouse name, address, and phone number.

1. In the Salesforce application, from Setup, click **Develop** > **Pages**.

2. Click **New**.

3. In the `Label` field, enter `FindNearbyWarehousesPage`.

   The `FindNearbyWarehousesPage` page is included in the package you installed, so if you're copying this code to create a new page, you'll want to name your page something different.

4. Select the `Available for Salesforce mobile apps` checkbox.

   Selecting this checkbox designates that the page is mobile-ready and can be used in Salesforce1.

5. Copy and paste this code into the Visualforce Markup tab.

   Line breaks in the code might cause errors, so you might need to delete some of the line breaks.

   ```
   <apex:page sidebar="false" showheader="false"
       standardController="Warehouse__c"
       recordSetVar="warehouses" extensions="FindNearby">

       <apex:includeScript value="{!$Resource.googleMapsAPI}" />
       <!-- This API key needs to be set up for there to be
           no JS errors -->
       <!--http://salesforcesolutions.blogspot.com/2013/01/
           integration-of-salesforcecom-and-google.html-->
       <!--<script type="text/javascript"
           src="https://maps.googleapis.com/
           maps/api/js?key=AIzaSyAVrfZm7_NhbL
           jHrFPdl242BYV1PBmDPqs&sensor=
           false"> </script>-->
   ```

```
<!-- Set up the map to take up the whole window -->
<style>
    html, body { height: 100%; }
    .page-map, .ui-content, #map-canvas
        { width: 100%; height:100%; padding: 0; }
    #map-canvas { height: min-height: 100%; }
</style>

<script>
    function initialize() {
        var lat, lon;

            // Check to see if the device has geolocation
            // detection capabilities with JS
            if (navigator.geolocation) {
                navigator.geolocation.getCurrentPosition(
                    function(position){
                    lat = position.coords.latitude;
                    lon = position.coords.longitude;

                    //Use VF Remoting to send values to be
                    //queried in the associated Apex Class
                    Visualforce.remoting.Manager.
                    invokeAction(
                        '{!$RemoteAction.FindNearby.
                            getNearby}',
                        lat, lon,
                        function(result, event){
                            if (event.status) {
                                console.log(result);
                                createMap(lat, lon, result);
                            } else if (event.type ===
                                'exception') {
                                //exception case code
                            } else {

                            }
                        },
                        {escape: true}
                    );
                });
            } else {
            //Set default values for map if the device
            //doesn't have geolocation capabilities
```

```
                    /** San Francisco **/
                    lat = 37.77493;
                    lon = -122.419416;

                    var result = [];
                    createMap(lat, lon, result);
            }

    }

    function createMap(lat, lng, warehouses){
        //Grab the map div and center the map at
        //the proper latitude/longitude
        var mapDiv = document.getElementById(
            'map-canvas');
        var map = new google.maps.Map(mapDiv, {
            center: new google.maps.LatLng(lat, lng),
            zoom: 12,
            mapTypeId: google.maps.MapTypeId.ROADMAP
        });

        //Set up the markers for the map using the
        //variable we queried for in our controller
        var warehouse;
        for(var i=0; i<warehouses.length;i++){
            warehouse = warehouses[i];
            console.log(warehouses[i]);
            setupMarker();
        }

    function setupMarker(){
        var content='<a href src="/'+ warehouse.Id +
            '" >'+
            warehouse.Name + '</a><br/>'+
            warehouse.Street_Address__c +
            '<br/>' + warehouse.City__c +
            '<br/>' + warehouse.Phone__c;

        //Create the callout that will pop up
        //on the marker
        var infowindow = new google.maps.
            InfoWindow({
            content: content
        });
```

```
                    //Place the marker
                    var marker = new google.maps.Marker({
                        map: map,
                        position: new google.maps.LatLng(
                            warehouse.Location__Latitude__s,
                            warehouse.Location__Longitude__s)
                    });

                    //Create an action to open the callout
                    google.maps.event.addListener(
                        marker, 'click', function(){
                        infowindow.open(map, marker);
                    });
                }
            }

            //Run the initialize function when the window loads
            google.maps.event.addDomListener(
                window, 'load', initialize);

        </script>

        <body style="font-family: Arial; border: 0 none;">
            <div id="map-canvas"></div>
        </body>
    </apex:page>
```

6. Click **Save**.

Now that we've created the Visualforce page for finding warehouses, the next step is to create a tab for it. We'll then add the page to the navigation menu in Salesforce1.

Create a New Tab

Now we'll create a new tab and add the Visualforce page you just created.

1. From Setup, click **Create** > **Tabs**.

2. In the Visualforce Tabs section, click **New**.

3. In the Visualforce Page drop-down list, select FindNearbyWarehousesPage, or the page you created in the previous step.

4. In the Tab Label field, enter *Find Warehouses*.

This label appears on the navigation menu in Salesforce1.

5. Click into the `Tab Style` field, and select the Globe style.

    The icon for this style appears as the icon for the page in the Salesforce1 navigation menu.

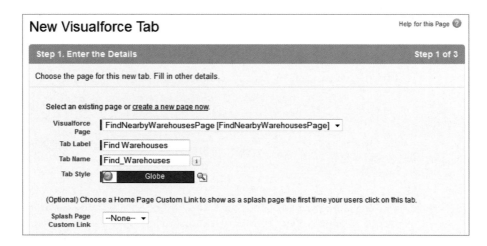

6. Click **Next**.

7. Click **Next** to accept the visibility defaults.

8. Deselect the **Include Tab** checkbox so that the tab isn't included in any of the apps in the organization. We only want this tab to appear when users are viewing it on their mobile device.

9. Click **Save**.

Now that you've created the Visualforce page and the tab, you're ready to add the new tab to the navigation menu.

Add the Tab to the Navigation Menu

In this step, we'll add the tab as a navigation menu item. It will instantly become available to Salesforce1 app users that have access to it.

1. From Setup, click **Mobile Administration** > **Mobile Navigation**.

2. Select Find Warehouses and click **Add** to move it over to the Selected list.

3. Click **Save**.

When your Salesforce1 users log in, they'll see the Find Warehouses menu item in the navigation menu. Now let's test it out.

Test Out the Visualforce Page

Now you'll play the part of an Acme Wireless mobile technician and search for nearby warehouses on your device.

1. Open the Salesforce1 app on your mobile device.

2. Tap ▤ to access the navigation menu.

   You should see **Find Warehouses** under the Apps section.

3. Tap **Find Warehouses**.

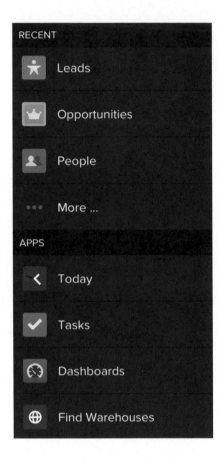

4. Click **OK** when you see a prompt that asks to use your current location. A map that contains all the nearby warehouse locations within 20 miles appears.

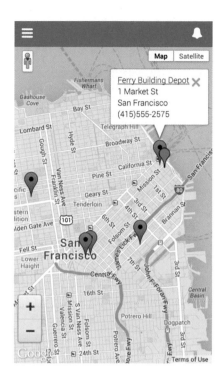

The warehouses in our package sample data are all located in the San Francisco area. If you're testing this from another location, be sure to add a warehouse located within 20 miles. To add a new warehouse, choose **Warehouse** from the Force.com app menu, click the Warehouses tab, and then click **New** in the Recent Warehouses section.

That's it! You can see how easy it is to make standard pages and tabs available to your mobile users.

For more information about development guidelines for Visualforce pages, see Visualforce Guidelines and Best Practices on page 171.

Tell Me More: Where Visualforce Pages Can Appear in Salesforce1

When you create a Visualforce page, you can make it available from a number of places in the Salesforce1 user interface.

- Navigation menu—Available when you tap ≣ from the Salesforce1 app.

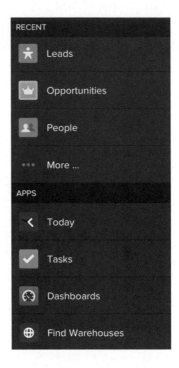

- Publisher—Available when you tap ⊞ from the Salesforce1 app.

- Record Home page (as a mobile card)—Available when you navigate to a record.

You can also reference, and link to, another Visualforce page in your Visualforce markup, using the `$Page` global, or in Apex custom code, by creating a `PageReference` object and returning it from an action method. Page references like this are common in multi-page processes. Be sure to select `Available for Salesforce mobile apps` for all pages in a multi-page process.

If a referenced page doesn't have `Available for Salesforce mobile apps` selected, it won't prevent the referencing, or parent, page from appearing in Salesforce1. However, when a user tries to access the non-mobile enabled page, they'll receive an "Unsupported Page" error message.

Tell Me More: About the Code

Let's take a look at some of the code behind our Visualforce page that finds warehouses.

FindNearby Apex Class Query

This snippet is a dynamic SOQL query that uses variables passed in from the Visualforce page to find warehouses within 20 miles of the device accessing the page. This page works on any mobile device and HTML5–enabled desktop browser.

If the page is unable to obtain the location, the search is centered on San Francisco. If you test this from a browser, you might have to approve that the page can access your location depending on your device security settings.

```
String queryString =
   'SELECT Id, Name, Location__Longitude__s,
    Location__Latitude__s, ' +
   Street_Address__c, Phone__c, City__c ' +
   'FROM Warehouse__c ' +
   'WHERE DISTANCE(Location__c,
   GEOLOCATION('+lat+','+lon+'), \'mi\') < 20 ' +
   'ORDER BY DISTANCE(Location__c,
   GEOLOCATION('+lat+','+lon+'), \'mi\') ' +
   'LIMIT 10';
```

Visualforce Page **initialize** Function

The `initialize` function in the Visualforce page uses the HTML5 geolocation API to get the coordinates of the user. The browser gets the position without using any plug-ins or external libraries, and then uses

JavaScript remoting to invoke the `getNearby` function in the Apex controller and passes in the coordinates.

```
function initialize() {
    var lat, lon;

    // Check to see if the device has geolocation
    // detection capabilities with JavaScript
    if (navigator.geolocation) {
        navigator.geolocation.getCurrentPosition(
            function(position){
            lat = position.coords.latitude;
            lon = position.coords.longitude;

            //Use VF Remoting to send values to be
            //queried in the associated Apex Class
            Visualforce.remoting.Manager.invokeAction(
                '{!$RemoteAction.FindNearby.getNearby}', lat, lon,
                function(result, event){
                    if (event.status) {
                        console.log(result);
                        createMap(lat, lon, result);
                    } else if (event.type === 'exception') {
                        //exception case code
                    } else {

                    }
                },
                {escape: true}
            );
        });
    } else {
    //Set default values for map if the device doesn't
    //have geolocation capabilities
        /** San Francisco **/
        lat = 37.77493;
        lon = -122.419416;

        var result = [];
        createMap(lat, lon, result);
    }
```

Visualforce Page Redirect Code

The page `FindNearbyWarehousesPage` uses the Google Maps JavaScript API v3 to plot the nearby warehouses on a map. We resize the map based on the records returned by the SOQL query and plot each record as marker on the map.

The most important piece of the code is where we determine whether or not the page is being viewed in the Salesforce1 app. If it is, the redirect link to the warehouse record must be coded slightly differently. If the page runs in the Salesforce1 app, we must use the `navigateToSobjectRecord` method to go to the record detail page but still stay in the app. We can check this with a simple try/catch construct, and then set the redirect link accordingly.

```
try{
    if(sforce.one){
    warehouseNavUrl =
        'javascript:sforce.one.navigateToSObject(
        \'' + warehouse.Id + '\')';
    }
} catch(err) {
    console.log(err);
    warehouseNavUrl = '\\' + warehouse.Id;
}

    var warehouseDetails =
        '<a href="' + warehouseNavUrl + '">' +
        warehouse.Name + '</a><br/>' +
        warehouse.Street_Address__c + '<br/>' +
        warehouse.City__c + '<br/>' +
        warehouse.Phone__c;
```

CHAPTER 12 Adding Functionality with Visualforce Custom Actions

In this chapter ...

- Custom Actions Scenario
- Try It Out: Create a Visualforce Custom Action
- Tell Me More: About the Code

Actions appear in the publisher in the Salesforce1 app, and are a quick way for mobile users to access commonly used tasks or functionality.

We learned about standard actions that can be configured with point-and-click tools in Using Actions in Salesforce1 on page 45. In this chapter we'll look at custom actions, which are actions that you define. There are two types of custom actions:

- Visualforce—specifies a Visualforce page that's called from the publisher.
- Canvas—specifies a canvas app that's called from the publisher. For more information about canvas custom actions, see Extending Salesforce1 with Canvas Custom Actions on page 104.

Custom actions aren't specific to mobile users, and appear in both the Salesforce1 app and in the full Salesforce site. In the Salesforce1 app, custom actions appear in the action tray. In the full Salesforce site, custom actions appear in the Chatter publisher.

Custom Actions Scenario

In this chapter, we'll further extend the Acme Wireless organization and give mobile technicians a way to quickly create an order. We'll create a Visualforce page and make it available as a custom action from the publisher. That way, if the technicians are out at a customer site and they want to order a part, they can quickly navigate to the page.

The custom action enables the technician to enter the part name and a radius, and the Visualforce page searches all warehouses within the given radius for that part. Once a warehouse is located, the technician simply enters the quantity and clicks a button to create the order. This is all done within the context of the customer account.

Try It Out: Create a Visualforce Custom Action

First, we'll create a Visualforce custom action that references a Visualforce page.

The custom action we're creating uses these elements from the package that you downloaded and installed for this guide.

- `QuickOrderPage` Visualforce page
- `QuickOrderController` Apex class
- `Mobile_Design_Templates` static resource used for styling the page

We'll take an in-depth look at the code later in this chapter. But first, we're going to create the action and try it out.

The Visualforce code for this page uses the location of the current customer account to find warehouses located within the specified distance (in miles) that also have a particular part in stock.

1. In the Salesforce application, from Setup, click **Customize** > **Accounts** > **Buttons, Links, and Actions**.
2. Click **New Action**.
3. In the Action Type drop-down list, select Custom Visualforce.
4. In the Visualforce Page drop-down list, select QuickOrderPage.
5. In the `Label` field, enter `Create Quick Order`.

   This is the action name that appears to the user in the publisher in the Salesforce1 app or in the publisher menu in the full Salesforce site.

6. Click **Save**.

Now that we've created the custom action, we'll add the action to the Account page layout. This ensures that the custom action appears in the publisher when you go to the page layout for a customer account.

Add the Visualforce Custom Action to the Page Layout

Now we'll add the custom action to the Account page layout.

1. From Setup, click **Customize** > **Accounts** > **Page Layouts**.

2. Click **Edit** next to the Warehouse Schema Account Layout.

3. Click the Actions category in the palette.

4. In the Publisher Actions section, click **override the global publisher layout**.

5. Drag the Create Quick Order element into the Publisher Actions section so that it appears as the first element on the left.

   Our mobile technicians are going to use this custom action a lot, and we're putting it at the start of the list so it'll be one of the first actions they see when they open the publisher.

6. Click **Save**.

Now that we've created the custom action and added it to the page layout, we're ready to see it in action.

Test Out the Visualforce Custom Action

Now you'll play the part of an Acme Wireless mobile technician on a customer call, and we'll test out the custom action in Salesforce1.

1. Open the Salesforce1 app on your mobile device.

2. Tap ▤ to access the navigation menu.

3. From the navigation menu, tap **Accounts** and navigate to an account.

4. Tap ➕ to access the publisher.

5. Tap **Create Quick Order**.

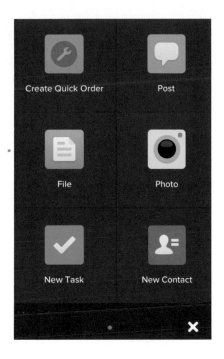

6. In the `Merchandise Name` field, enter the name of an item, such as *iPhone 5*.

7. In the `Max Delivery Distance (miles)` field, enter *10*.

8. Tap **Submit**.

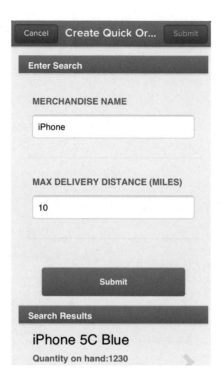

9. In the Search Results section at the bottom, you'll see a list of merchandise that matches what you searched for. The list shows parts contained in warehouses within 10 miles of the current account. Tap iPhone 5S Gold.

10. In the `Quantity` field, enter `1`.

    After identifying nearby warehouses that contain the part you're looking for, this screen lets you enter a quantity and creates an order for the part. The order is associated with the current account.

    💡 Tip: If you want to return to the search screen, be sure to use the **Back** button. If you tap **Cancel**, an invoice with no line items is created.

11. Tap **Submit**.

    The order has been created. Swipe to the third page indicator, and you'll see the Invoices related list. Tap the Invoices related list, and you'll see the new invoice. You can tap the invoice and then tap **Line Items** on the Related page to see the line item that was created for the iPhone 5S Gold part.

Success! You've gone through the entire process of enabling a mobile technician to quickly search for a part in a warehouse and create an order.

For more information about development guidelines for Visualforce page, see Visualforce Guidelines and Best Practices on page 171.

Tell Me More: About the Code

There are two code objects behind our Visualforce custom action: the Apex class `QuickOrderController` and the Visualforce page `QuickOrderPage`.

The Apex class is the controller for the Visualforce page, and uses the `@RemoteAction` annotation on the methods. When you use this annotation, the Visualforce page wraps the logic in a JavaScript-friendly way. This is known as *Visualforce remoting*.

Visualforce remoting allows for quick and tight integration between Apex and JavaScript. This communication model works asynchronously as opposed to the synchronous model in the traditional Visualforce/Apex MVC paradigm. So after passing parameters into your controller, you can get the result from a response handler function, and write any additional client-side logic before doing any DOM manipulation or building your page with mobile templates or frameworks.

Visualforce remoting is ideal for mobile developers on the Salesforce1 Platform because it simplifies the direct server-side access to Salesforce objects and allows you to use Apex tools such as SOQL, Apex methods, and so on for rapid platform development. And, you don't have to deal with view state, which makes pages perform better.

Apex Class `QuickOrderController`

This class uses Visualforce remoting and contains the logic called by the Visualforce page to find warehouses and create orders and line items.

```
global class QuickOrderController{
    public static List<Merchandise__c> merchandise;
    public static Line_Item__c quickOrder;


    public QuickOrderController(ApexPages.
        StandardController controller){
    }

    @RemoteAction
    global static List<Merchandise__c> findWarehouses(String accId,
        String merchName, String warehouseDist){
        merchandise = new List<Merchandise__c>();
        String queryString = '';
```

```
Account acc = [Select Location__Longitude__s,
Location__Latitude__s, Name, Id
from Account where Id =: accId];

//Finds warehouses nearby if you have location
//specified on the Account
if(acc.Location__Latitude__s != null &&
    acc.Location__Longitude__s != null){
    queryString = 'SELECT Id, (SELECT Id, Name, Quantity__c,

        Warehouse__r.Name, Warehouse__r.Id,
        Warehouse__r.Street_Address__c,
        Warehouse__r.City__c '+
        'FROM Merchandise__r WHERE Name
        like \'%'+merchName+'%\') '
        +'FROM Warehouse__c WHERE '
        +'DISTANCE(Location__c, GEOLOCATION('
        +acc.Location__Latitude__s+','
        +acc.Location__Longitude__s+'), \'mi\')';
    if(warehouseDist != null){
        queryString += ' <'+ warehouseDist;
    }

}
//If no location defined on the Account, this will run
//query against the merchandise name only
else {
    queryString = 'SELECT Id, Name,
        Location__Longitude__s,
        Location__Latitude__s, '
        +'(SELECT Id, Name, Warehouse__r.Name,
        Quantity__c
        FROM Merchandise__r WHERE Name
        like \'%'+merchName+'%\') '
        +'FROM Warehouse__c limit 25';

}

//This creates a list of merchandise
//to display in the search results
Warehouse__c[] warehouses = Database.Query(queryString);
for(Warehouse__c warehouse : warehouses){
    Merchandise__c[] merch =
```

```
            warehouse.getSObjects('Merchandise__r');
            if (merch != null) {
                for (Merchandise__c m : merch){
                    merchandise.add(m);
                }
            }
        }
    return merchandise;

}


//This remote action creates the invoice for the quick order
@RemoteAction
global static Line_Item__c createQuickOrder(
    String accId, String merchandiseId){
    Invoice__c newInvoice = new Invoice__c();
    newInvoice.Account__c = accId;
    insert newInvoice;

    quickOrder = new Line_Item__c();
    Merchandise__c m = [Select Id, Name from Merchandise__c
        where Id=: merchandiseId limit 1];
    quickOrder.Merchandise__c = m.Id;
    quickOrder.Invoice__c = newInvoice.Id;

    return quickOrder;
}


//This remote action creates the line item related to the
//invoice for the quick order
@RemoteAction
global static Boolean insertQuickOrder(String o, String q){
    try {
        Integer quantity = integer.valueof(q);

    Line_Item__c order = new Line_Item__c();
    /* The order variable being passed in as a param is being
    passed in the form of a JSON object. You need to use
    the JSON deserialize method in Apex to convert it
    into a SObject */
    order = (Line_Item__c)JSON.deserialize(
        o, Line_Item__c.class);

    order.Quantity__c = quantity;
```

```
    insert order;

//Need to requery for the name for the post to chatter
//since it wasn't explicitly specified
Line_Item__c li = [Select Name, Merchandise__r.Name, Id,
    Quantity__c, Invoice__c from Line_Item__c
    where Id =: order.Id];

    FeedItem post = new FeedItem();
    post.ParentId = aId;
  post.Body = UserInfo.getName() + ' just created a quick order';

    post.type = 'LinkPost';
    post.LinkUrl = '/' + li.Invoice__c;
    post.Title = li.Merchandise__r.Name + ': ' + li.quantity__c;
    insert post;
} catch(System.Exception ex) {
    system.debug(ex.getMessage());
}
    return true;
}


//This remote action handles deleting the invoice if
//the user doesn't want to insert the line item
@RemoteAction
global static Boolean goBack(String invoiceId){
    // Delete created invoice and return to original
    //search screen
    Invoice__c cancelledInvoice = [select Id from Invoice__c
        where Id=: invoiceId];
    delete cancelledInvoice;

    return true;
}

}
```

The Apex controller also has an `insertQuickOrder` method that creates a feed item about the new order in the account feed as shown in this code snippet. The feed item is a link post that links to the invoice.

```
FeedItem post = new FeedItem();
post.ParentId = aId;
post.Body = UserInfo.getName() + ' just created a quick order';
post.type = 'LinkPost';
```

```
    post.LinkUrl = '/' + li.Invoice__c;
    post.Title = li.Merchandise__r.Name + ': ' + li.quantity__c;
    insert post;
```

Visualforce Page `QuickOrderPage`

This page calls the controller with the user input and then displays the merchandise and warehouse information to the user. If the user wants to create an order, this page also calls the controller to create the order associated with the customer account and add a line item. At the beginning of the page, the code also does some styling of the page using the Salesforce mobile design templates.

```
<apex:page standardController="Account"
    extensions="QuickOrderController" docType="html-5.0"
   standardStylesheets="false"    showheader="false" sidebar="false">


    <!--Include stylesheets for the mobile look and feel -->
    <apex:stylesheet value="{!URLFOR(
        $Resource.Mobile_Design_Templates,
        'Mobile-Design-Templates-master/
            common/css/app.min.css')}"/>
    <apex:includeScript value="{!URLFOR(
        $Resource.Mobile_Design_Templates,
        'Mobile-Design-Templates-master/common/js/
            jQuery2.0.2.min.js')}"/>
    <apex:includeScript value="{!URLFOR(
        $Resource.Mobile_Design_Templates,
        'Mobile-Design-Templates-master/common/js/
            jquery.touchwipe.min.js')}"/>
    <apex:includeScript value="{!URLFOR(
        $Resource.Mobile_Design_Templates,
        'Mobile-Design-Templates-master/common/
            js/main.min.js')}"/>

      <style>
          /* Default S1 color styles */
          .list-view-header, .data-capture-buttons a {
                background: -webkit-linear-gradient(
                    #2a93d5,#107abb);
                background: linear-gradient(#2a93d5,#107abb);
                box-shadow: 0 1px 3px rgba(0,0,0,.2),
                    inset 0 1px 0 rgba(255,255,255,.21);
```

```
              color: white;
              font-weight: bold;
        }

        #resultPage, #searchPage {
            padding-bottom: 50px;
        }
    </style>
```

The `QuickOrderPage` also calls the Force.com Canvas SDK to enable the publisher **Submit** button and close the publisher window.

First, it includes a reference to the SDK:

```
<!-- This needs to be included so the publisher can be used
    to submit the action -->
<script type='text/javascript'
src='/canvas/sdk/js/publisher.js'></script>
```

Then it calls the `setValidForSubmit` method to enable the publisher **Submit** button:

```
//This method will activate the publish button
//so the form can be submitted
Sfdc.canvas.publisher.publish({
    name: "publisher.setValidForSubmit",
    payload:"true"});
```

After the `setValidForSubmit` is called and the user clicks **Submit**, this `subscribe` method fires. This method invokes the final JavaScript function which uses JavaScript remoting to insert the line item (thus completing the quick order) and then post a feed item to the account:

```
<script type='text/javascript'>
    Sfdc.canvas.publisher.subscribe({name: "publisher.post",
        onData:function(e) {
    //This subscribe fires when the user hits
    //Submit in the publisher
    insertQuickOrder();
    }});
</script>
```

Finally, after the callback from the remoting method returns successfully, this method closes the publisher window:

```
// Success - close the publisher and refresh the feed
Sfdc.canvas.publisher.publish({name: "publisher.close",
    payload:{ refresh:"true"}});
```

CHAPTER 13 Integrating Your Web Applications in Salesforce1 with Force.com Canvas

In this chapter ...

- About Force.com Canvas
- Extending Salesforce1 with Canvas Custom Actions
- Extending Salesforce1 with Canvas Apps in the Feed

Force.com Canvas lets you easily integrate a third-party Web application in Salesforce1.

The Force.com Canvas SDK is an open-source suite of JavaScript libraries that provide simple methods that use existing Salesforce1 APIs (REST API, SOAP API, Chatter REST API) so you can build a seamless end-user experience for your mobile users.

About Force.com Canvas

Force.com Canvas features include:

- Language Independence—You develop it and we display it. With Force.com Canvas you can develop in the language of your choice and easily surface the app inside of the Salesforce1 app.

    The third-party app that you want to expose as a canvas app can be written in any language. The only requirement is that the app has a secure URL (HTTPS).

- JavaScript SDK—Lightweight and easy-to-use JavaScript libraries allow your app to authenticate and communicate without having to deal with cross-domain network issues. This gives your users a single command center to drive all their apps.

- Simplified Authentication—Allows you to authenticate by using OAuth 2.0 or a signed request. This means that your app can connect to Salesforce at the data layer while remaining seamless for users.

- App Registration and Management—Developers can create apps and allow their customers to install them with a single click. Administrators can easily install apps from developers, and quickly manage who in their organizations can use the app.

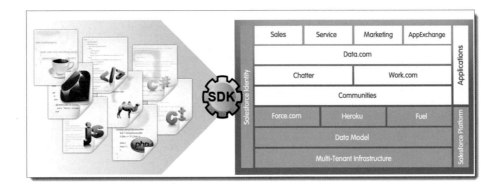

Extending Salesforce1 with Canvas Custom Actions

Canvas custom actions appear in the publisher in the Salesforce1 app, and provide a way to make canvas apps available from the publisher.

In this chapter, we'll further extend the Acme Wireless organization by integrating a third-party app with the platform using Force.com Canvas. Acme Wireless has a Web application running on Heroku called

Shipify. They use it to process orders. We'll copy the Shipify application that runs on Heroku and make it available as a canvas custom action from the publisher.

In this scenario, warehouse workers with mobile devices can bring up a list of open customer orders. They can select an order and then process it for shipping. After the order is processed, Shipify sets the order status in Salesforce and posts a feed item to the associated customer account. You'll see how easy it is to integrate a Web application and enable it to communicate with Salesforce. This creates a seamless experience for your mobile users.

Try It Out: Clone the Shipify Web Application

We'll start the process of creating a canvas custom action by cloning the Shipify Web application.

In addition to the prerequisites for this book listed in Development Prerequisites on page 69, you'll also need:

- "Customize Application" and "Modify All Data" user permissions. If you're an administrator, you most likely already have these permissions. Otherwise, you need to add them so that you can see the Canvas App Previewer and create canvas apps.

- Git installed. Go here to install and configure Git:
  `https://help.github.com/articles/set-up-git.`

  After you install Git, you might need to configure SSH by using the keygen tool. See `https://help.github.com/articles/generating-ssh-keys` for more information. If you're using Windows, this tool is located in the Git `\bin` directory, which isn't added to the path after you install Git. Add the `\bin` directory to your path by using Control Panel. Depending on your installation directory, the path might be something like `C:\Program Files (x86)\Git\bin.`

- A GitHub account to clone the code example. Go here to set up a GitHub account:
  `https://github.com/plans.`

- A Heroku account because our Web application will run on Heroku. Go here to create a Heroku account:
  `https://api.heroku.com/signup.`

- Heroku Toolbelt to manage the Heroku app from the command line. Go here to download and install Heroku Toolbelt: `https://toolbelt.heroku.com.`

Shipify is a Web application that Acme Wireless uses to track the status of customer orders, customer shipments, and deliveries. The warehouse workers use this application to check for outstanding orders, fulfill those orders, and then update the shipping status. The Shipify Web application contains some order processing logic, but it's not a full order processing application. Its purpose is to demonstrate how you can integrate your Web applications with the Salesforce1 app.

Shipify is a Node.js application that runs on Heroku. Each running instance of the application must reference the consumer secret for the connected app that you create in your organization. Therefore, you'll need to have your own instance of Shipify on Heroku that you can then add as a canvas app. In this step, we'll clone the application, which is the first step in the process.

1. Open a command window and navigate to the directory where you want to download Shipify. When you clone the application, it will create a directory called `Shipify-Node-App` from wherever you run the clone command.

   - From a computer running Windows, open a command window by clicking **Start** > **Run...** and entering in `cmd`.

   - From a computer running Mac OS, open a command window by pressing Command + Space and entering `terminal`.

2. Enter this command: `git clone https://github.com/forcedotcom/Shipify-Node-App`

3. Navigate to the `Shipify-Node-App` directory. For example, if your `Shipify-Node-App` directory is located in `C:\Users\yourname,` you would enter this command: `cd C:\Users\yourname\Shipify-Node-App`

4. Enter this command to log in to Heroku: `heroku login`

   When prompted, enter your email and password.

5. Enter this command to create a new Heroku app: `heroku apps:create`

   Confirmation that the app was created looks like this:

   ```
   Creating deep-samurai-7923... done, stack is cedar
   http://deep-samurai-7923.herokuapp.com/ |
   git@heroku.com:deep-samurai-7923.git
   Git remote heroku added
   ```

6. Copy the URL of the Heroku app because we'll use it in the next task. In this example, the URL is `http://deep-samurai-7923.herokuapp.com`, but you'll want to copy the URL of your own Heroku app. Your URL must begin with `https://`.

   We've created the Shipify Web application in Heroku, but it won't work yet because we still need to deploy it, which we'll do in a later step.

The next step is to add it as a canvas app in Salesforce.

Create the Shipify Canvas App

In this step, we'll expose the Shipify Web application as a canvas app.

You'll need user permissions "Customize Application" and "Modify All Data" to create a canvas app.

1. In the Salesforce application, from Setup, click **Create** > **Apps**.

2. In the Connected Apps related list, click **New**.

3. In the `Connected App Name` field, enter *Shipify*.

4. In the `Contact Email` field, enter your email address.

5. In the API (Enable OAuth Settings) section, select `Enable OAuth Settings`.

6. In the `Callback URL` field, paste the URL of the Heroku app you just created and change the protocol to `HTTPS`. For example, your final URL should look something like `https://deep-samurai-7923.herokuapp.com`.

7. In the `Selected OAuth Scopes` field, select Full access and click **Add**.

   As a best practice, you'll want to keep the OAuth scopes as limited as needed for your canvas app functionality.

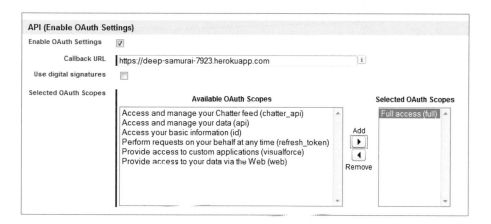

8. In the Canvas App Settings section, select `Force.com Canvas`.

9. In the `Canvas App URL` field, enter the same URL you entered in the `Callback URL` field with `/signedrequest` appended to it. For example, the URL might look like `https://deep-samurai-7923.herokuapp.com/signedrequest`.

10. In the Access Method drop-down list, select Signed Request (POST).

11. In the `Locations` field, select Chatter Tab and Publisher and click **Add**.

    For a canvas app to appear in the publisher, you only need to specify a location of Publisher. In this scenario, we also chose Chatter Tab to be able to easily test the canvas app by looking at the Chatter tab.

12. Select `Create Actions Automatically`.

Selecting this field creates a global custom action for the canvas app.

```
▼    Canvas App Settings

        Force.com Canvas    ☑

        Canvas App URL    https://immense-dusk-1701.herokuapp.com/signedrequest

        Access Method    Signed Request (POST) ▼

   SAML Initiation Method ⓘ    None                        ▼

            Locations                 Available                      Selected

                              Chatter Feed          ▲        Chatter Tab  ▲
                              Console                        Publisher
                              Layouts and Mobile Cards   Add
                              Mobile Nav               ▶
                              Open CTI                 ◀
                              Visualforce Page        Remove



        Lifecycle Class ⓘ    [                ] 🔍

   Enable as a Canvas Personal App ⓘ  ☐

   Create Actions Automatically ⓘ  ☑

      Hide Publisher Header ⓘ  ☐

   Hide Publisher Share Button ⓘ  ☐


                              Save   Cancel
```

13. Click **Save**. After the canvas app is saved, the detail page appears.

We added the canvas app, and now we'll specify who can access it.

Configure Who Can Access the Shipify Canvas App

You've created the canvas app, but no one can see it until you configure user access.

1. From Setup, click **Manage Apps** > **Connected Apps**.

2. Click the Shipify app, and then click **Edit**.

3. In the Permitted Users drop-down list, select **Admin approved users are pre-authorized**. Click **OK** on the pop-up message that appears.

4. Click **Save**.

   Now you'll define who can see your canvas app. This can be done using profiles and permission sets. In this example, we'll allow anyone with the System Administrator profile to access the app.

5. Click **Shipify** in the Master Label column on the Connected Apps page.

6. In the Profiles related list on the Connected App Detail page, click **Manage Profiles**.

7. Select the `System Administrator` profile and click **Save**.

That's it! The next step is to set up some environment variables on Heroku.

Configure the Heroku Environment Variables

Now that we've created the canvas app, we need to set up an environment variable for the consumer secret.

1. From Setup, click **Create** > **Apps**.

2. In the Connected Apps related list, click **Shipify**.

3. Next to the `Consumer Secret` field, click the link **Click to reveal**.

4. Copy the consumer secret.

5. Open a command window, navigate to the `Shipify-Node-App` directory, and enter this command to create the environment variable: `heroku config:add APP_SECRET='`***`Your_Consumer_Secret`***`'`

   If you're working from a Windows computer, you may need to replace the single quotes with double quotes (").

6. Enter this command: `heroku config:add RUNNING_ON_HEROKU='true'`

   This specifies that the application is running on Heroku. This is helpful for testing so you don't need to re-deploy every time you make a change. If you're working from a Windows computer, you may need to replace the single quotes with double quotes (").

7. Enter this command to deploy the app to Heroku: `git push heroku master`

   If the process completes successfully, you'll see something like this:

   ```
   -----> Compiled slug size: 11.2MB
   -----> Launching... done, v6
          http://deep-samurai-7923.herokuapp.com deployed to Heroku

   To git@heroku.com:deep-samurai-7923.git
    * [new branch]      master -> master
   ```

   If you receive a "permission denied" error message, you may need to set up your SSH key and add it to Heroku. See `https://devcenter.heroku.com/articles/keys`.

You can quickly test that the canvas app is working in the full Salesforce site by clicking the Chatter tab. Click the **Shipify** link on the left, and you'll see the Heroku application appear right in Salesforce and display a list of open orders, including the one you created in the previous chapter. Now we'll add the canvas custom action to the publisher layout so our users can see it.

Add the Action to the Global Publisher Layout

When we created the canvas app, we opted to automatically create the action. In this step, we'll add the action to the global publisher layout so it shows up in the publisher in the Salesforce1 app.

1. In the Salesforce application, from Setup, click **Create** > **Global Actions** > **Publisher Layouts**.

2. Click **Edit** next to the Global Layout.

   This is the default layout for the publisher.

3. Drag the Shipify element into the Publisher Actions section so that it appears as the first element on the left.

   Our warehouse workers are going to use this custom action a lot, so we're putting it at the start of the list so it'll be one of the first actions they see when they open the publisher.

   > Note: The canvas custom action was created automatically, so it used the name of the canvas app for the name of the action (in this case, Shipify). In a production scenario, you'll want to change the action name to represent what the user can do. For example, we could change the name of this action to Ship Orders.

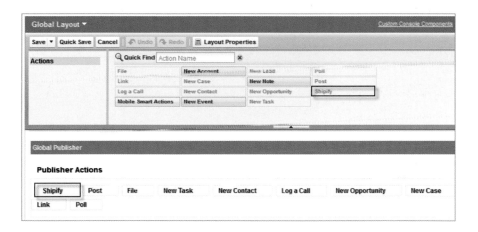

4. Click **Save**.

Now that we've created the custom action and added it to the publisher layout, we're ready to see it in action (no pun intended).

Test Out the Canvas Custom Action

Now you'll play the part of an Acme Wireless warehouse worker processing orders, and we'll test out the custom action in the Salesforce1 app.

1. On your mobile device, tap ➕ to access the publisher.

2. Tap **Shipify**.

    A list of all open invoices along with the customer account and warehouse information appears.

3. Tap one of the invoices, and a screen appears that shows the total amount of the invoice and a **Ship It** button.

4. Tap **Ship It**.

    This kicks off order processing in the Shipify Web application. In addition, Shipify sets the invoice status to Closed and creates a feed item for the account that shows that the invoice has shipped along with the related order number and a link to the invoice.

You did it! You've gone through the entire process of integrating a Web application in the Salesforce1 app using Force.com Canvas and canvas custom actions. Now warehouse workers can find customer orders, ship them out, and then update the order and the account feed.

For more information about development guidelines for canvas apps in the publisher, see **Canvas Apps in the Publisher** on page 206.

Tell Me More: Get Context in your Canvas App

The Force.com Canvas SDK provides calls and objects that let you retrieve context information about the application and the current user from Salesforce.

Getting Context

When you authenticate your canvas app using signed request, you get the CanvasRequest object (which contains the Context object) as part of the POST to the canvas app URL. If you're authenticating using OAuth, or if you want to make a call to get context information, you can do so by making a JavaScript call.

You can use this information to make subsequent calls for information and code your app so that it appears completely integrated with the Salesforce1 user interface.

The following code sample is an example of a JavaScript call to get context. This code creates a link with the text "Get Context" which then calls the `Sfdc.canvas.client.ctx` function.

```
<script>
    function callback(msg) {
        if (msg.status !== 200) {
            alert("Error: " + msg.status);
            return;
        }
        alert("Payload: ", msg.payload);
    }

    var ctxlink = Sfdc.canvas.byId("ctxlink");
    var client = Sfdc.canvas.oauth.client();
    ctxlink.onclick=function() {
        Sfdc.canvas.client.ctx(callback, client)};
    }
</script>

<a id="ctxlink" href="#">Get Context</a>
```

Context Objects

When you make a call to get context in your canvas app, you get a CanvasRequest object back in the response. This object contains all the contextual information about the application and the user. The context objects include:

Object	Description
CanvasRequest	Returns the Context and Client objects.
Client	Returns context information about the client app.
Context	Returns information about the consumer of the canvas app. Contains the Application, Environment, Links, Organization, and User objects.
Application	Returns information about the canvas app, such as version, access method, URL, and so on.
Environment	Returns information about the environment, such as location, UI theme, and so on.

Object	Description
Links	Returns links, such as the metadata URL, user URL, Chatter groups URL, and so on. You can use these links to make calls into Salesforce from your app.
Organization	Returns information about the organization, such as name, ID, currency code, and so on.
User	Returns information about the currently logged-in user, such as locale, name, user ID, email, and so on.

This code snippet shows an example of the CanvasRequest object:

```
{
    "context":
    {
        "application":
        {
            "applicationId":"06Px000000003ed",
            "authType":"SIGNED_REQUEST",
            "canvasUrl":"http://instance.salesforce.com:8080
                /canvas_app_path/canvas_app.jsp",
            "developerName":"my_java_app",
            "name":"My Java App",
            "namespace":"org_namespace",
            "referenceId":"09HD00000000AUM",
            "samlInitiationMethod": "None",
            "version":"1.0.0"
        },
        "user":
        {
            "accessibilityModeEnabled":false,
            "currencyISOCode":"USD",
            "email":"admin@6457617734813492.com",
            "firstName":"Sean",
            "fullName":"Sean Forbes",
            "isDefaultNetwork":false,
            "language":"en_US",
            "lastName":"Forbes",
            "locale":"en_US",
            "networkId":"0DBxx000000001r",
            "profileId":"00ex0000000jzpt",
            "profilePhotoUrl":"/profilephoto/005/F",
```

```
    "profileThumbnailUrl":"/profilephoto/005/T",
    "roleId":null,
    "siteUrl":"https://mydomain.force.com/",
    "siteUrlPrefix":"/mycommunity",
    "timeZone":"America/Los_Angeles",
    "userId":"005x0000001SyyEAAS",
    "userName":"admin@6457617734813492.com",
    "userType":"STANDARD"
},
"environment":
{
    "parameters":
    {
        "complex":
        {
            "key1":"value1",
            "key2":"value2"
        },
        "integer":10,
        "simple":"This is a simple string.",
        "boolean":true
    },
    "dimensions":
    {
        "height": "900px",
        "width": "800px",
        "maxHeight":"2000px",
        "maxWidth":"1000px",

        "clientHeight":"80px",
        "clientWidth":"968px"
    },
    "displayLocation":"Chatter",
    "locationUrl": "http://www.salesforce.com
        /some/path/index.html",
    "uiTheme":"Theme3",
    "record":{},
    "version":
    {
        "api":"32.0",
        "season":"SUMMER"
    },
},
```

```
        "organization":
        {
            "currencyIsoCode":"USD",
            "multicurrencyEnabled":true,
            "name":"Edge Communications",
            "namespacePrefix":"org_namespace",
            "organizationId":"00Dx00000001hxyEAA"
        },
        "links":
        {
            "chatterFeedItemsUrl":"/services/data/v32.0/
                chatter/feed-items",
            "chatterFeedsUrl":"/services/data/v32.0/
                chatter/feeds",
            "chatterGroupsUrl":"/services/data/v32.0/
                chatter/groups",
            "chatterUsersUrl":"/services/data/v32.0/
                chatter/users",
            "enterpriseUrl":"/services/Soap/c/32.0/
                00Dx00000001hxy",
            "loginUrl":"http://login.salesforce.com",
            "metadataUrl":"/services/Soap/m/32.0/00Dx00000001hxy",
            "partnerUrl":"/services/Soap/u/32.0/00Dx00000001hxy",
            "queryUrl":"/services/data/v32.0/query/",
            "recentItemsUrl":"/services/data/v32.0/recent/",
            "restUrl":"/services/data/v32.0/",
            "searchUrl":"/services/data/v32.0/search/",
            "sobjectUrl":"/services/data/v32.0/sobjects/",
            "userUrl":"/005x0000001SyyEAAS"
        }
    },
    "client":
    {
        "instanceId":"06Px000000002JZ",
        "instanceUrl":"http://instance.salesforce.com:
            8080",
        "oauthToken":"00Dx0000X00Or4J!ARQAKowP65p8FDHkvk.Uq5...",
        "targetOrigin":"http://instance.salesforce.com:
            8080"
    },
"algorithm":"HMACSHA256",
"userId":"005x0000001SyyEAAS",
```

```
"issuedAt":null
 }
```

For more information about context objects and the Force.com Canvas SDK, see the *Force.com Canvas Developer's Guide*.

Extending Salesforce1 with Canvas Apps in the Feed

Force.com Canvas enables you to add even more functionality to the feed by exposing your canvas apps as feed items in the Salesforce1 app.

You can use this functionality to:

* Post to the feed from a canvas app exposed from a canvas custom action in the publisher or post to the feed through the Chatter API.

* Display a canvas app directly inside a feed item.

In this chapter, we'll further extend the Acme Wireless organization by integrating a third-party Web app in the feed using Force.com Canvas.

Acme Wireless has a Web application that runs on Heroku called DeliveryTrakr that they use to process deliveries of customer orders. We'll copy the DeliveryTrackr application that runs on Heroku and make it available as a global action from the publisher.

In this scenario, warehouse workers equipped with mobile devices can bring up a list of deliveries. When warehouse workers access the app from the publisher, they can use it to create feed posts of different types. The app can create a text post which is a feed item that contains information about a delivery, a link post which is a feed item that contains a link to the DeliveryTrakr app, or a canvas post which is a feed item that contains a link to another canvas app. The user can click on this link to access a canvas app that lets them approve or deny a delivery.

Try It Out: Clone the DeliveryTrakr Web Application

We'll start the process of integrating a canvas app in the feed by cloning the DeliveryTrakr Web application

In addition to the prerequisites for this book listed in Development Prerequisites on page 69, you'll also need:

* "Customize Application" and "Modify All Data" user permissions. If you're an administrator, you most likely already have these permissions. Otherwise, you need to add them so that you can see the Canvas App Previewer and create canvas apps.

* Git installed. Go here to install and configure Git:
  `https://help.github.com/articles/set-up-git`.

After you install Git, you might need to configure SSH using the keygen tool. See `https://help.github.com/articles/generating-ssh-keys` for more information. If you're using Windows, this tool is located in the Git `\bin` directory, which isn't added to the path after you install Git. Add the `\bin` directory to your path by using Control Panel. Depending on your installation directory, the path might be something like: `C:\Program Files (x86)\Git\bin`.

- A GitHub account to clone the code example. Go here to set up a GitHub account: `https://github.com/plans`.

- A Heroku account because our Web application will run on Heroku. Go here to create a Heroku account: `https://api.heroku.com/signup`.

- Heroku Toolbelt to manage the Heroku app from the command line. Go here to download and install Heroku Toolbelt: `https://toolbelt.heroku.com`.

The steps to create and run a canvas app are the same, regardless of the app's functionality. So the steps in this chapter are similar to those of the previous chapter, Extending Salesforce1 with Canvas Custom Actions on page 104.

DeliveryTrakr is a Web application that Acme Wireless uses to track deliveries of customer orders. The warehouse workers use this application to check for orders that have been delivered and post delivery information to the feed. The DeliveryTrakr Web application contains some delivery processing logic, but it's not a full application. Its purpose is to demonstrate how you can integrate your Web applications with the Salesforce1 app.

DeliveryTrakr is a Java application that runs on Heroku. Each running instance of the application must reference the consumer secret for the connected app that you create in your organization. Therefore, you'll need to have your own instance of DeliveryTrakr on Heroku that you can then add as a canvas app. In this step, we'll clone the application, which is the first step in the process.

1. Open a command window and navigate to the directory where you want to download DeliveryTrakr. When you clone the application, it will create a directory called `Delivery-Tracker-Java-App` from wherever you run the clone command.

    - From a computer running Windows, open a command window by clicking **Start** > **Run...** and entering in *cmd*.

    - From a computer running Mac OS, open a command window by pressing Command + Space and entering *terminal*.

2. Enter the command: `git clone https://github.com/forcedotcom/Delivery-Tracker-Java-App`

3. Navigate to the `Delivery-Tracker-Java-App` directory. For example, if your `Delivery-Tracker-Java-App` directory is located in `C:\Users\yourname`, you

would enter this command: `cd`
`C:\Users\yourname\Delivery-Tracker-Java-App`

4. Enter this command to log in to Heroku: `heroku login`

   When prompted, enter your email and password.

5. Enter this command to create a new Heroku app: `heroku apps:create`

   Confirmation that the app was created looks like this:

```
Creating deep-samurai-7923... done, stack is cedar
http://deep-samurai-7923.herokuapp.com/ |
git@heroku.com:deep-samurai-7923.git
Git remote heroku added
```

6. Copy the URL of the Heroku app because we'll use it in the next task. In this example, the URL is `http://deep-samurai-7923.herokuapp.com`, but you'll want to copy the URL of your own Heroku app.

   We've created the DeliveryTrakr Web application in Heroku, but it won't work yet because we still need to deploy it, which we'll do in a later step.

The next step is to add it as a canvas app in Salesforce.

Create the DeliveryTrakr Canvas App

In this step, we'll expose the DeliveryTrakr Web application as a canvas app.

You'll need user permissions "Customize Application" and "Modify All Data" to create a canvas app.

1. In the Salesforce application, from Setup, click **Create** > **Apps**.

2. In the Connected Apps related list, click **New**.

3. In the `Connected App Name` field, enter *DeliveryTrakr*.

4. In the `Contact Email` field, enter your email address.

5. In the API (Enable OAuth Settings) section, select `Enable OAuth Settings`.

6. In the `Callback URL` field, paste the URL of the Heroku app you just created and change the protocol to `HTTPS`. For example, your final URL might look something like `https://deep-samurai-7923.herokuapp.com`.

7. In the `Selected OAuth Scopes` field, select Full access and click **Add**.

   As a best practice, you'll want to keep the OAuth scopes as limited as needed for your canvas app functionality.

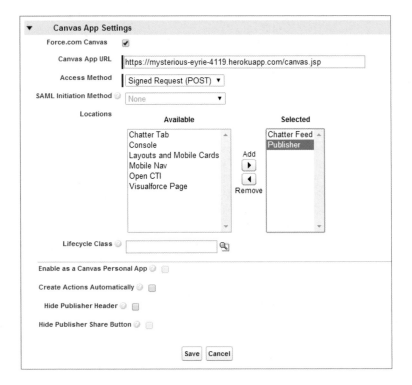

8. In the Canvas App Settings section, select `Force.com Canvas`.

9. In the `Canvas App URL` field, enter the same URL you entered in the `Callback URL` field with `/canvas.jsp` appended to it. For example, the URL might look like `https://deep-samurai-7923.herokuapp.com/canvas.jsp`.

10. In the Access Method drop-down list, select Signed Request (POST).

11. In the `Locations` field, select Chatter Feed and Publisher and click **Add**.

    We selected these values because the canvas app appears in the publisher as well as in the feed.

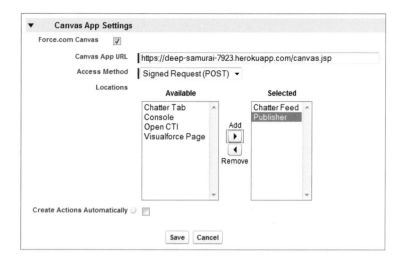

12. Click **Save**. After the canvas app is saved, the detail page appears.

We added the canvas app, and now we'll specify who can access it.

Configure Who Can Access the DeliveryTrakr Canvas App

You've created the canvas app, but no one can see it until you configure user access.

1. From Setup, click **Manage Apps** > **Connected Apps**.

2. Click the DeliveryTrakr app, and then click **Edit**.

3. In the Permitted Users drop-down list, select **Admin approved users are pre-authorized**. Click **OK** on the pop-up message that appears.

4. Click **Save**.

    Now you'll define who can see your canvas app. This can be done using profiles and permission sets. In this example, we'll allow anyone with the System Administrator profile to access the app.

5. On the Connected App Detail page, in the Profiles related list, click **Manage Profiles**.

6. Select the `System Administrator` profile and click **Save**.

That's it! The next step is to set up some environment variables on Heroku.

Configure the Heroku Environment Variables

Now that we've created the canvas app, we need to set up an environment variable for the consumer secret.

1. From Setup, click **Create** > **Apps**.

2. In the Connected Apps related list, click **DeliveryTrakr**.

3. Next to the `Consumer Secret` field, click the link **Click to reveal**.

4. Copy the consumer secret.

5. Open a command window, navigate to the `Delivery-Tracker-Java-App` directory, and enter this command to create the environment variable: `heroku config:add` `APP_SECRET='`***Your_Consumer_Secret***`'`

    If you're working from a Windows computer, you may need to replace the single quotes with double quotes (").

6. Navigate to the `Delivery-Tracker-Java-App\src\main\webapp\scripts` directory.

7. Open `shipment.js` in an editor. In the `onGetPayload` function, replace YOUR_APP_URL with the URL of your DeliveryTrakr app on Heroku: `p.url =` `"https://[YOUR_APP_URL]/signed-request.jsp?shipment=" +` `shipment;`

    This code is located on or around line 231. Using our example, the line of code should look like:

    ```
    p.url = "https://deep-samurai-7923.herokuapp.com/
        signed-request.jsp? shipment=" + shipment;
    ```

8. Save the changes to `shipment.js` and navigate back to the `Delivery-Tracker-Java-App` directory.

9. Enter this command: `heroku config:add RUNNING_ON_HEROKU='true'`

    This specifies that the application is running on Heroku. This is helpful for testing so you don't need to re-deploy every time you make a change. If you're working from a Windows computer, you may need to replace the single quotes with double quotes (").

10. Enter this command to get the file ready to commit: `git add —A`

11. Enter this command to commit the changes along with a comment: `git commit —m` `'`***MyChangeComments***`'`

    If you're working from a Windows computer, you may need to replace the single quotes with double quotes (").

12. Enter this command to deploy the app to Heroku: `git push heroku master`

If the process completes successfully, you'll see something like this:

```
-----> Compiled slug size: 11.2MB
-----> Launching... done, v6
       http://deep-samurai-7923.herokuapp.com deployed to Heroku

To git@heroku.com:deep-samurai-7923.git
 * [new branch]      master -> master
```

If you receive a "permission denied" error message, you may need to set up your SSH key and add it to Heroku. See `https://devcenter.heroku.com/articles/keys`.

You can quickly test that the canvas app is working from Setup in the full Salesforce site by clicking **Canvas App Previewer**. Click the **DeliveryTrakr** link on the left, and you'll see the Heroku application running in the previewer and displaying a list of shipments and their delivery status. Now we'll create a global action for the canvas app so that your mobile users can starting using what you've created.

Create a Global Action

We'll create a global action for the DeliveryTrakr app so that we can then add it to the global publisher layout.

In the previous canvas example, we selected `Create Actions Automatically` when we created the canvas app in Salesforce. So the global action was created for us. In this scenario, we didn't select that field, so we'll step through creating the action manually.

1. If the Canvas Previewer is still open, click **Close**. From Setup, click **Create** > **Global Actions** > **Actions**.

2. Click **New Action**.

3. In the Action Type drop-down list, select Custom Canvas.

4. In the Canvas App drop-down list, select DeliveryTrakr.

5. In the `Label` field, enter `Track Deliveries`.

   This is the label that appears to the user in the publisher in the Salesforce1 app or in the publisher menu in the full Salesforce site.

6. Click **Save**.

Now that we've created the global action, we'll add the action to the global publisher layout. This ensures that the action appears in the publisher where mobile users can access it.

Add the Action to the Global Publisher Layout

We just created the global action for the canvas app so now we'll add the action to the global publisher layout. Then it will appear in the publisher in the Salesforce1 app.

1. From Setup, click **Create** > **Global Actions** > **Publisher Layouts**.

2. Click **Edit** next to the Global Layout.

    This is the default layout for the publisher.

3. Drag the Track Deliveries element into the Publisher Actions section so that it appears as the first element on the left.

    Our warehouse workers are going to use this custom action a lot, so we're putting it at the start of the list so it'll be one of the first actions they see when they open the publisher.

4. Click **Save**.

Now that we've created the custom action and added it to the publisher layout, we're ready to see it in action.

Test Out the DeliveryTrakr Canvas App

Now you'll play the part of an Acme Wireless warehouse worker processing deliveries, and we'll test out the canvas app in the Salesforce1 app.

The DeliveryTrakr app demonstrates how a canvas app can create one of three types of posts in the feed:

*   Text post—Feed item that contains information about a delivery.
*   Link post—Feed item that contains a link to the DeliveryTrakr app.
*   Canvas post—Feed item that contains a link to another canvas app. This app is used by warehouse workers to approve or deny a delivery.

1. On your mobile device, tap **Feed** from the navigation menu.
2. Tap ➕ to access the publisher.

3. Tap **Track Deliveries**.

    The DeliveryTrakr app displaying a list of shipments appears.

4. Tap one of the deliveries in the grid.

5. Tap **Text Post**.

    You can also add some of your own text to the post by entering it in the **What are you working on?** pane.

6. Tap **Share**.

    This creates a text feed post about the shipment, and that post appears in the current user's feed.

7. To test out creating a link post, tap  and then **Track Deliveries**.

8. Tap one of the deliveries in the grid.

9. Tap **Link Post**.

   You can also add some of your own text to the post by entering it in the **What are you working on?** pane.

10. Tap **Share**.

This creates a link feed post about the shipment, and that post appears in the current user's feed. When you click the link, it brings you to the DeliveryTrakr app running on Heroku.

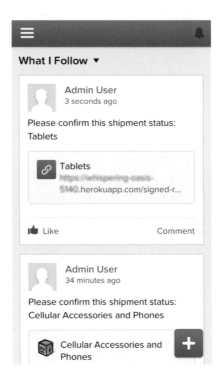

11. To test out creating a canvas post, tap 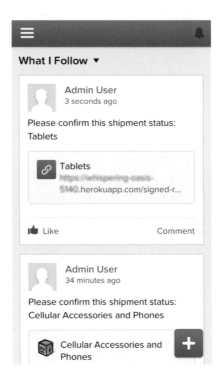 and then **Track Deliveries**.

12. Tap one of the deliveries in the grid.

13. Tap **Confirmation Post**.

    You can also add some of your own text to the post by entering it in the **What are you working on?** pane.

14. Tap **Share**.

    This creates a canvas feed post about the shipment with a link. When you click the link, it actually takes you to a canvas app where you can complete or cancel a shipment.

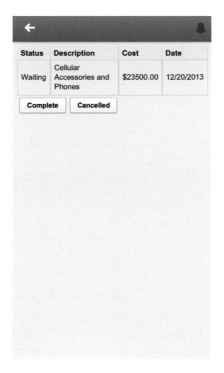

You did it! You've gone through the entire process of creating a canvas app that posts a text feed item, a link feed item, and—most importantly—a canvas app in the feed.

For more information about development guidelines for canvas apps in the feed, see Canvas Apps in the Feed on page 208.

Tell Me More: About the Code to Create Feed Items

In the code for the DeliveryTrakr Web application, the `shipment.js` file contains the logic to create the various feed items.

Creating a Canvas Feed Item

This code snippet from the `onGetPayload` function creates a feed item of type `CanvasPost`. As you can see, it dynamically sets all the post values and retrieves information about the canvas app, such as the `namespace` and `developerName`, from the signed request. You can also pass in parameters that are appended to the URL and used in the canvas app feed item.

```
else if ("approval" === action)
{
    p.feedItemType = "CanvasPost";
    p.auxText = "Please confirm this shipment status: " +
        shipments[shipment].description;
    p.namespace =  sr.context.application.namespace;
    p.developerName =  sr.context.application.developerName;
    p.thumbnailUrl = "https://cdn1.iconfinder.com/data/icons/
        VISTA/project_managment/png/48/deliverables.png";
    p.parameters =  "{\"shipment\":\"" + shipment + "\"}";
    p.title = shipments[shipment].description;
    p.description = "This is a travel shipment for Shipment - " +
        shipments[shipment].description +
        ".  Click the link to open the canvas app.";
}
```

Enabling the Share Button

This code snippet is from the `draw` function. After this statement is called, the Share button is enabled. This ensures that the user can't create a feed item until they have selected all the required elements for the canvas app.

```
$$.client.publish(sr.client, {
    name : 'publisher.setValidForSubmit',
    payload : true});
```

Publishing the Feed Item

When the user clicks the Share button, this code snippet publishes the feed item to the feed. The type of feed item it creates depends on which type you select: text, link, or canvas.

```
$$.client.publish(sr.client, {name : 'publisher.setPayload',
    payload : p});
```

CHAPTER 14 Calling Actions from the API

In this chapter ...

- Try It Out: Create an Invoice Action
- Tell Me More: Actions and the REST API

You can further extend the power of actions by calling them from the REST API.

Throughout this guide, we've seen how powerful actions are because they let you quickly extend the Salesforce1 app and give users the functionality they need right within the publisher. You can harness this power outside of the Salesforce1 app by calling actions from the REST API.

In this chapter, we'll walk through creating an action off the Invoice object and calling it from the Shipify Web application. After we make our changes, when users access the Shipify canvas app and click **Ship It**, the app will add a delivery record in Salesforce.

 Note: This chapter builds on the tasks completed in the section Extending Salesforce1 with Canvas Custom Actions on page 104. Be sure to complete the steps of downloading the Shipify Web application and creating the canvas app before starting the tasks in this chapter.

Try It Out: Create an Invoice Action

In this step, we'll create the Invoice action that adds the delivery record.

1. In the Salesforce application, from Setup, click **Create** > **Objects**.

2. Click Invoice.

3. Scroll down to the Buttons, Links, and Actions related list and click **New Action**.

4. In the Action Type drop-down list, select Create a Record.

5. In the Target Object drop-down list, select Delivery.

6. In the `Label` field, enter `Create Delivery`.

   The action name defaults to Create_Delivery. This is name by which the action is referenced by the API.

7. Click **Save**.

8. After you save the action, the page layout editor appears. Drag the Invoice, Order Number, and Owner fields to the page layout.

9. Click **Save**.

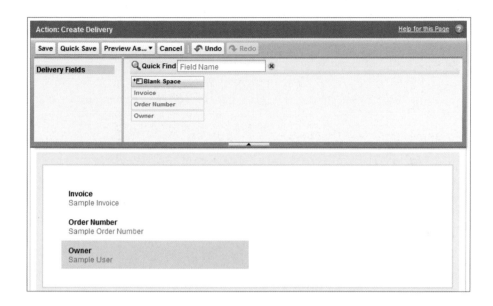

Now that we've created the action, we'll add the code to the Shipify Web application that's running on Heroku.

Add the Code to Call the Action

We'll add the code that calls the `Create_Delivery` action by using the REST API.

1. Navigate to the `Shipify-Node-App` directory where you downloaded the Shipify Web application. Copy the file `shipment_with_action_api_call.js` to file `shipment.js`.

   - On a Windows computer, the command would be: `copy shipment_with_action_api_call.js shipment.js`
   - On a Mac OS computer, the command would be: `cp shipment_with_action_api_call.js shipment.js`

2. Confirm that you want to overwrite `shipment.js`.

3. Enter this command to get the files ready to commit: `git add —A`

4. Enter this command to commit the changes along with a comment: `git commit —m '`***MyChangeComments***`'`

   If you're working from a Windows computer, you may need to replace the single quotes with double quotes (").

5. Enter this command to deploy the app to Heroku: `git push heroku master`

👁 **Example:** If you look at the code in `shipment.js` that creates the delivery record, you'll see that it passes the invoice ID and does a `POST` to the `/quickActions/Create_Directory` resource.

```
Shipment.prototype.createDelivery = function createDelivery(so) {

    var self = this;
    var authorization = this._formatAuthHeader(so.authorization);

    if(!so.invoiceId) {
        var err = new Error("Must Pass InvoiceId to Ship!");
        err.statusCode = '400';
        err.err = err.message;
        this.emit('create-delivery', err);
        return;
    }
    var quickActionBody = {
        contextId: so.invoiceId,
        record: {
            Order_Number__c: so.orderNumber
        }
    };

    var deliveryReq = {
        url: so.instanceUrl + '/services/data/v29.0/
            sobjects/Invoice__c/quickActions/Create_Delivery/',
        method: 'POST',
        headers: {
            'Authorization': authorization,
            'Content-Type': 'application/json'
        },
        body: JSON.stringify(quickActionBody)
    };

    //Make Ajax request and emit 'create-delivery'
    //with result data or error back to listner.
    request(deliveryReq, this.handleAJAXResponse(
        'create-delivery'));
};
```

We've got our API call all ready to go, so let's test it out by shipping a customer order.

Test Out Calling the Action from the API

Now we'll test out the code that calls the action and adds a delivery record in the Salesforce1 app.

1. From your mobile device, tap  to access the publisher.

2. Tap **Shipify**.

   A list of all open invoices along with the customer information appears.

3. Tap one of the invoices. A screen appears that shows the total amount of the invoice and a **Ship It** button.

4. Tap **Ship It**.

    This kicks off order processing in the Shipify Web application. Shipify sets the invoice status to Closed and creates a feed item for the account. But now, a delivery record is also created for the invoice. After the order is shipped, you'll see a confirmation screen.

5. Tap **Cancel**.

    In the feed, you'll see the new delivery record

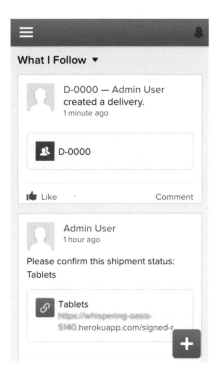

6. To see the closed invoice, tap ☰ and then tap **Accounts**.

7. Tap the account for the shipped order and swipe to the first indicator page. You'll see a feed item that lets the user know the order has been shipped.

Voila! You've now gone through the process of updating the Shipify Web application to make a REST API call to invoke the action that you created.

Tell Me More: Actions and the REST API

The REST API contains a number of resources and calls that you can use when working with actions.

Publisher Quick Actions

Use the Publisher Quick Actions resource to return a list of actions as well as custom fields and objects that appear in the feed. The resource uses a URI of the format
`services/data/v32.0/quickActions/`.

You might have a preferred tool for working with Salesforce APIs. If you don't have a preferred tool, Workbench is an easy way to get started. You can find information about Workbench at https://developer.salesforce.com/page/Workbench. You can find information about the REST API in the *Force.com REST API Developer's Guide*.

Global Actions

To return global actions, use: `services/data/v32.0/quickActions/`

A call to this resource returns information about the global actions including our Shipify canvas custom action as shown in this snippet of the response.

```
...
    {
    "urls" : {
        "quickAction" : "/services/data/v32.0/
            quickActions/LogACall",
        "defaultValues" : "/services/data/v32.0/
            quickActions/LogACall/defaultValues",
        "describe" : "/services/data/v32.0/
            quickActions/LogACall/describe"
        },
            "name" : "LogACall",
            "type" : "LogACall",
            "label" : "Log a Call"
    },
    {
    "urls" : {
        "quickAction" : "/services/data/v32.0/
            quickActions/Shipify",
        "describe" : "/services/data/v32.0/
            quickActions/Shipify/describe"
        },
            "name" : "Shipify",
            "type" : "Canvas",
            "label" : "Shipify"
        },
...
```

Object Actions

To return a specific object's actions, as well as global actions, use:
`services/data/v32.0/sobjects/`***object***`/quickActions/`

The call `/services/data/v32.0/sobjects/Invoice__c/quickActions` returns information about global actions as well as the Invoice `Create Delivery` action, as shown in this snippet of the response.

```
...
    { "urls" : {
        "quickAction" : "/services/data/v32.0/
```

```
              quickActions/Shipify",
        "describe" : "/services/data/v32.0/
              quickActions/Shipify/describe"
    },
    "name" : "Shipify",
    "type" : "Canvas",
    "label" : "Shipify"
    },
    {
    "urls" : {
        "defaultValuesTemplate" : "/services/data/v32.0/
              sobjects/Invoice__c/quickActions/Create_Delivery/
              defaultValues/{ID}",
        "quickAction" : "/services/data/v32.0/
              sobjects/Invoice__c/quickActions/Create_Delivery",
        "defaultValues" : "/services/data/v32.0/
              sobjects/Invoice__c/quickActions/Create_Delivery/
              defaultValues",
        "describe" : "/services/data/v32.0/
              sobjects/Invoice__c/quickActions/Create_Delivery/
              describe"
    },
        "name" : "Invoice__c.Create_Delivery",
        "type" : "Create",
        "label" : "Create Delivery"
    },
...
```

Specific Actions

To return a specific action, use:

`services/data/v32.0/sobjects/`***object***`/quickActions/`***Action_Name***

The call `/services/data/v32.0/sobjects/Invoice__c/` `quickActions/Create_Delivery` returns information about only the `Create_Delivery` action, as shown in this response.

```
{
    "colors": [
        {
            "theme": "theme4",
            "color": "AA8E0A",
            "context": "primary"
        },
        {
```

```
            "theme": "theme3",
            "color": "AA8E0A",
            "context": "primary"
        }
    ],
    "miniIconUrl": "https://instance.salesforce.com/img/
        icon/custom51_100/truck16.png",
    "sourceSobjectType": "Invoice__c",
    "targetParentField": "Invoice__c",
    "targetRecordTypeId": null,
    "targetSobjectType": "Delivery__c",
    "visualforcePageName": null,
    "iconUrl": "https://instance.salesforce.com/img/
        icon/custom51_100/truck32.png",
    "iconName": null,
    "canvasApplicationName": null,
    "height": null,
    "icons" : [ ],
...
    "layout": {
        "layoutRows": [{
            "layoutItems": [
                {
                    "layoutComponents": [{
                        "details": {
                            "namePointing": false,
                            "custom": true,
                            "htmlFormatted": false,
                            "dependentPicklist": false,
                            "calculatedFormula": null,
                            "defaultValueFormula": null,
                            "defaultedOnCreate": false,
                            "digits": 0,
                            "groupable": true,
                            "permissionable": false,
                            "referenceTo": ["Invoice__c"],
                            "relationshipOrder": 0,
                            "soapType": "tns:ID",
                            "nameField": false,
                            "sortable": true,
                            "filterable": true,
                            "restrictedPicklist": false,
                            "caseSensitive": false,
```

```
                              "calculated": false,
                              "scale": 0,
                              "nillable": false,
                              "externalId": false,
                              "idLookup": false,
                              "controllerName": null,
                              "deprecatedAndHidden": false,
                              "inlineHelpText": null,
                              "writeRequiresMasterRead": false,
                              "createable": true,
                              "updateable": false,
                              "relationshipName": "Invoice__r",
                              "autoNumber": false,
                              "unique": false,
                              "picklistValues": [],
                              "displayLocationInDecimal": false,
                              "cascadeDelete": true,
                              "restrictedDelete": false,
                              "length": 18,
                              "name": "Invoice__c",
                              "type": "reference",
                              "defaultValue": null,
                              "byteLength": 18,
                              "label": "Invoice",
                              "precision": 0
                          },
                          "displayLines": 1,
                          "tabOrder": 1,
                          "value": "Invoice__c",
                          "type": "Field"
                      }],
                      "placeholder": false,
                      "editable": true,
                      "required": true,
                      "label": "Invoice"
                  },
                  {
                      "layoutComponents": [],
                      "placeholder": true,
                      "editable": false,
                      "required": false,
                      "label": ""
                  }
              ],
```

146

```
                "numItems": 2
        }],
        "useCollapsibleSection": false,
        "useHeading": false,
        "columns": 2,
        "heading": null,
        "rows": 1
    },
    "defaultValues": [],
    "width": null,
    "urls": {
        "defaultValuesTemplate": "/services/data/v32.0/
            sobjects/Invoice__c/quickActions/
            Create_Delivery/defaultValues/{ID}",
        "quickAction": "/services/data/v32.0/
            sobjects/Invoice__c/quickActions/Create_Delivery",
        "defaultValues": "/services/data/v32.0/
            sobjects/Invoice__c/quickActions/
            Create_Delivery/defaultValues",
        "describe": "/services/data/v32.0/
            sobjects/Invoice__c/quickActions/
            Create_Delivery/describe"
    },
    "name": "Invoice__c.Create_Delivery",
    "type": "Create",
    "label": "Create Delivery"
}
```

Action Details

To return a specific action's descriptive detail, use:

services/data/v32.0/sobjects/***object***/quickActions/***Action_Name***/describe/

Action Default Values and Field Values

To return a specific action's default values, including default field values, use:

services/data/v32.0/sobjects/***object***/quickActions/***Action_Name***/defaultValues/

The call `/services/data/v32.0/sobjects/Invoice__c/`
`quickActions/Create_Data/defaultValues` returns information about defaults for
the Invoice `Create_Delivery` action, as shown in this snippet of the response.

```
...
{
    "attributes":{
        "type":"Delivery__c"
```

```
       }
   }
   ...
```

Action Default Values

To return the default values for an action, use: `/services/data/v32.0/subjects/` **object**`/quickActions/`**Action_Name**`/defaultValues/`**Parent_ID**

Describe Layouts

Use the global describe layouts resource to get global layout information for objects, including action objects. The resource uses a URI of the format: `services/data/v32.0/ sobjects/Global/describe/layouts/`

A call to this resource returns layout information for the global actions (including our Shipify canvas custom action), as shown in this response.

```
{
    "recordTypeSelectorRequired":[
        false
    ],
    "recordTypeMappings":[

    ],
    "layouts":[
        {
            "relatedLists":[

            ],
            "relatedContent":null,
            "detailLayoutSections":[

            ],
            "editLayoutSections":[

            ],
            "multirowEditLayoutSections":[

            ],
            "offlineLinks":[

            ],
            "buttonLayoutSection":null,
```

```
"highlightsPanelLayoutSection":null,
"quickActionList":{
    "quickActionListItems":[
        {
            "quickActionName":"Shipify",
            "colors":[

            ],
            "miniIconUrl":null,
            "targetSobjectType":null,
            "iconUrl":null,
            "urls":{
                "quickAction":"/services/data/v32.0/
                    quickActions/Shipify",
                "describe":"/services/data/v32.0/
                    quickActions/Shipify/describe"
            },
            "icons":[

            ],
            "type":"Canvas",
            "label":"Shipify"
        },
        {
            "quickActionName":"FeedItem.TextPost",
            "colors":[

            ],
            "miniIconUrl":null,
            "targetSobjectType":null,
            "iconUrl":null,
            "urls":{

            },
            "icons":[

            ],
            "type":"Post",
            "label":"Post"
        },
        {
            "quickActionName":"FeedItem.ContentPost",
            "colors":[
```

```
                             ],
                             "miniIconUrl":null,
                             "targetSobjectType":null,
                             "iconUrl":null,
                             "urls":{

                             },
                             "icons":[

                             ],
                             "type":"Post",
                             "label":"File"
                          },
                          {
                             "quickActionName":"NewTask",
                             "colors":[
                                {
                                   "color":"44A12C",
                                   "theme":"theme4",
                                   "context":"primary"
                                },
                                {
                                   "color":"1797C0",
                                   "theme":"theme3",
                                   "context":"primary"
                                }
                             ],
                             "miniIconUrl":"https://instance.
                                salesforce.com/img/icon/tasks16.png",
                             "targetSobjectType":"Task",
                             "iconUrl":"https://instance.
                                salesforce.com/img/icon/home32.png",
                             "urls":{
                                "quickAction":"/services/data/v32.0/
                                   quickActions/NewTask",
                                "defaultValues":"/services/data/v32.0/
                                   quickActions/NewTask/defaultValues",
                                "describe":"/services/data/v32.0/
                                   quickActions/NewTask/describe"
                             },
                             "icons":[
                                {
                                   "url":"https://instance.
```

```
                    salesforce.com/img/icon/home32.png",
            "height":32,
            "theme":"theme3",
            "width":32,
            "contentType":"image/png"
        },
        {

            "url":"https://instance.
                salesforce.com/img/icon/tasks16.png",
            "height":16,
            "theme":"theme3",
            "width":16,
            "contentType":"image/png"
        },
        ...
    ],
    "type":"Create",
    "label":"New Task"
},
{
    "quickActionName":"NewContact",


        ...
    ],
    "type":"Create",
    "label":"New Contact"
},
...
    "type":"Create",
    "label":"New Lead"
},
{

    "quickActionName":"FeedItem.LinkPost",
    "colors":[

    ],
    "miniIconUrl":null,
    "targetSobjectType":null,
    "iconUrl":null,
    "urls":{

    },
    "icons":[
```

```
                ],
                "type":"Post",
                "label":"Link"
            },
            {

                "quickActionName":"FeedItem.PollPost",
                "colors":[

                ],
                "miniIconUrl":null,
                "targetSobjectType":null,
                "iconUrl":null,
                "urls":{

                },
                "icons":[

                ],
                "type":"Post",
                "label":"Poll"
            }
        ]
    },
    "id":"00hR0000000MpLAIA0"
    }
  ]
}
```

Use the describe layouts resource to obtain a description of a layout for a specific object, including action objects. The resource uses a URI of the format: `services/data/ v32.0/sobjects/`***object***`/describe/layouts/`

CHAPTER 15 Extending the User Interface with Flexible Pages

In this chapter ...

- What is a Flexible Page?
- Flexible Pages: The Big Picture
- Deploying a Flexible Page
- About Flexible Page Tabs
- Making Your Flexible Page Available in Salesforce1
- Tell Me More: Flexible Pages

In this chapter, we'll extend the Acme Wireless organization for a different mobile audience. In our scenario, Acme Wireless maintains a central warehouse where all the repair parts and accessories are stored. The storefront locations order parts from the warehouse so that they can keep some inventory on hand. When they need a special part that's not in stock, storefronts can special order it from the warehouse.

Instead of focusing on the mobile technicians like we have for most of this book, this time we're going to shift our attention to the delivery drivers transporting inventory from the warehouse to the storefronts. Currently, the drivers use a custom app to create, update, and track their deliveries. We're going to use a Flexible Page to create a home page for that app, which will allow us to incorporate it into Salesforce1. This way, the drivers have a single source for information they need to manage their deliveries.

153

What is a Flexible Page?

A Flexible Page is a type of custom mobile layout, designed to help you customize specific pages in Salesforce1.

Flexible Pages occupy a middle ground between page layouts and Visualforce pages. Like a page layout, Flexible Pages allow you to add custom items to a page. However, they don't have the same structure as a page layout, and the custom items are all components.

You can use a Flexible Page to create a home page for a custom app—an App Page— that you can then add directly into the Salesforce1 mobile navigation. This provides your Salesforce1 users with a mobile home page that enables them to quickly access the objects and items that are most important in that app.

You can also assign global actions to a Flexible Page by specifying them in the Flexible Page XML. When users tap ➕ from a Flexible Page, any global actions that you've assigned to it will show up in the publisher.

About Flexible Pages

A Flexible Page consists of a list of a single region, named "main", containing *ComponentInstances*. A ComponentInstance contains a set of properties for an instance of a particular component, such as which component the instance points to, and a set of name/value pairs representing a subset of the component's attributes.

Available Components

Not every component can be specified in a ComponentInstance. Even among those that are allowed, not all of their attributes can be specified. Currently, two components are supported for use in Flexible Pages.

`flexipage:filterListCard`
   Points to a list view and displays the first few records from that view.

   The `flexipage:filterListCard` component supports all list views that are associated with standard and custom objects except:

   - Activity
   - ContentVersion (Files)
   - Task
   - User
   - UserProfile

`flexipage:recentItems`
   A list of most recently used items that supports these objects, based on the specified properties:

- All custom objects
- All standard objects for which both of these conditions are true:
  - A compact layout is defined for the object.
  - The object is tracked in the most recently used objects list.

  If an object is tracked in the most recently used objects list, one or both of the `LastViewedDate` or `LastReferencedDate` fields will be present.

The Recent Items component doesn't support these objects:

- ContentVersion (Files)
- User
- UserProfile

`flexipage:reportChart`

The Report Chart component gives you the ability to include a chart from a report in your Flexible Page.

Properties:

- label: If you leave this property blank, the component label is taken from the label of the report instead.
- reportName: the API name of the report

This component is supported in API version 32.0 and later and won't work with reports that are located in the My Personal Custom Reports folder. If you include them in a package, Report Chart components that refer to reports in the Unfiled Public Reports folder aren't deployable.

`flexipage:richText`

The Rich Text component gives you the ability to add text, simple HTML markup, and images to your Flexible Page.

Properties:

- richTextValue: the HTML or text to display

   Note: JavaScript, CSS, iframes, and other advanced markup aren't supported in the Rich Text component. If you need to use advanced HTML elements in a component, we recommend that you use a Visualforce page component.

The Rich Text component is limited to 4,000 characters. It supports `.png`, `.gif`, and `.jpg` image formats. This component is supported in API version 32.0 and later.

`flexipage:visualforcePage`

The Visualforce Page component gives you the ability to include a Visualforce page in your Flexible Page.

155

Properties:

- label: the component label. If you leave this property blank, the component label is taken from the label of the Visualforce page.

- pageName: the API name of the Visualforce page to render

- height: the height of the Visualforce page in pixels. This value must be a whole number, and not negative. If this property is left blank, a default height of 300 pixels is assigned.

This component is supported in API version 32.0 and later.

A Visualforce page that you want to include as a component must have the `Available for Salesforce mobile apps` checkbox selected so that it will appear in Salesforce1. This checkbox is available for pages that are set to API version 27.0 and later.

So, what can a Flexible Page contain?

Flexible Pages can include:

- Components that display list views, recent items, a report chart, rich text, or a Visualforce page
- Global Chatter actions

Flexible Pages: The Big Picture

It's not enough to just create the XML for the Flexible Page. After you create it, you've got to deploy it to your organization, configure the page, and get it into Salesforce1. Here's an overview of the steps from beginning to end:

1. Before creating your page, consider which components you need to include and what global actions your users will need.

2. Create the Flexible Page XML file.

3. Add global actions to your page, whether they're out-of-the-box global actions from Salesforce or ones that you create yourself.

   You can assign specific global actions to your Flexible Page in the XML for the page. If you don't define specific actions in the XML, the action bar won't appear on the page.

4. Deploy the Flexible Page into your development organization.

5. Create a Flexible Page custom tab.

6. Add your Flexible Page tab to the Salesforce1 navigation menu.

We'll walk through all these tasks, starting with step 2, in this chapter. But before we can get started, we need to download the custom Deliveries app that the delivery drivers have been using.

Before We Begin: Download the Deliveries App

As we mentioned previously, Acme Wireless delivery drivers use a custom app to create, update, and track their deliveries. We want to add a Flexible Page to it so we can surface it in Salesforce1, but before we can do that, we need to download the custom app.

1. Go to
   `https://github.com/forcedotcom/Salesforce1-Dev-Guide-Setup-Package`.

2. Click **Download ZIP**.

3. Save the `Salesforce1-Dev-Guide-Setup-Package.zip` to your hard drive.

4. Extract the `Salesforce1-Dev-Guide-Setup-Package.zip` file.

   In it, you'll find `Salesforce1_Dev_Guide_Deliveries_App.zip`.

5. Now extract the `Salesforce1_Dev_Guide_Deliveries_App.zip` file.

Remember where you extracted the Deliveries app files, because we'll be returning there shortly.

Creating a Flexible Page

You create a Flexible Page manually in XML, then deploy it into Salesforce either through the Force.com Migration Tool, the Force.com IDE, or Workbench.

The Flexible Page layout and style is provided by Salesforce. There's no custom coding necessary.

Here's a sample of what a Flexible Page XML file looks like. This is our Deliveries app starting code, which we'll work with in the next exercise.

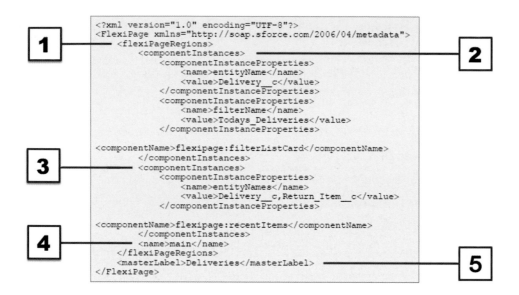

1. Start of the Flexible Page region. Flexible Pages can have only one region.

2. Start of the `componentInstances` properties.

3. Start of the `flexipage:filterListCard` component.

4. Name of the region. Must be "main".

5. Master label of the Flexible Page.

Ready to give it a shot? Let's create one for ourselves.

Try It Out: Create a Flexible Page

As we mentioned, we have to create our Flexible Page manually as an XML file. You'll need an XML editor for this task and the next one.

In the `Salesforce1_Dev_Guide Deliveries_App` folder created when you extracted the package, you'll see a `flexipages` folder. Inside, you'll find a sample version of the final Flexible Page file we're creating here, for your reference. But you're going to create one for yourself. Let's get coding!

1. Open the XML editor of your choice.

2. Open a new file.

3. Copy and paste this code block into your XML editor:

```xml
<?xml version="1.0" encoding="UTF-8"?>
<FlexiPage xmlns="http://soap.sforce.com/2006/04/metadata">
```

```
        <flexiPageRegions>
            <componentInstances>
                <componentInstanceProperties>
                    <name>entityName</name>
                    <value>Delivery__c</value>
                </componentInstanceProperties>
                <componentInstanceProperties>
                    <name>filterName</name>
                    <value>Todays_Deliveries</value>
                </componentInstanceProperties>

<componentName>flexipage:filterListCard</componentName>
            </componentInstances>
            <componentInstances>
                <componentInstanceProperties>
                    <name>entityNames</name>
                    <value>Delivery__c,Return_Item__c</value>
                </componentInstanceProperties>
                <componentName>flexipage:recentItems</componentName>

            </componentInstances>
            <name>main</name>
        </flexiPageRegions>
        <masterLabel>Deliveries</masterLabel>
</FlexiPage>
```

4. Save the file as `Deliveries.flexipage` in the `flexipages` folder.

    ⊘ **Important**: Always save your Flexible Pages with the `.flexipage` extension.

All right, we've created a basic Flexible Page, but there's another block of code we need to add: a section specifying actions to be assigned to the Flexible Page. We're not done with the XML just yet.

Assigning Actions to A Flexible Page

We learned all about actions in the Using Actions in Salesforce1 chapter, where we created and configured an action using point-and-click tools. Actions you want to use for your Flexible Pages must first be created and configured in the full Salesforce site, but unlike objects, where you add the action to a page layout declaratively, actions on Flexible Pages must be specified in the XML.

Only global actions are supported for Flexible Pages.

When a user accesses actions from the Flexible Page in Salesforce1, only the actions that you specify for the Flexible Page are displayed.

In this exercise, we'll be adding a pre-configured global action to the Flexible Page. This action lets our drivers schedule a delivery while on the road.

Try It Out: Add an Action to Your Flexible Page

A global action called "New Delivery" for this Flexible Page is included in the sample app package you downloaded at the start of this chapter. We just need to call it in the XML.

1. If it's not already open, re-open the `Deliveries.flexipage` file in your XML editor.

2. Add this action codeblock to the end of the XML, just before the `</FlexiPage>` tag.

   This codeblock associates the New Delivery action with the Flexible Page.

   ```
   <quickActionList>
       <quickActionListItems>
           <quickActionName>New_Delivery</quickActionName>
       </quickActionListItems>
   </quickActionList>
   ```

3. Save the `Deliveries.flexipage` file.

Now, when users open the Deliveries app from the Salesforce1 menu, the Flexible Page will have a ➕ that they can tap to open the publisher and access this action.

👁 **Example:** Your full codeblock should look like this:

```
<?xml version="1.0" encoding="UTF-8"?>
<FlexiPage xmlns="http://soap.sforce.com/2006/04/metadata">
    <flexiPageRegions>
        <componentInstances>
            <componentInstanceProperties>
                <name>entityName</name>
                <value>Delivery__c</value>
            </componentInstanceProperties>
            <componentInstanceProperties>
                <name>filterName</name>
                <value>Todays_Deliveries</value>
            </componentInstanceProperties>
          <componentName>flexipage:filterListCard</componentName>

        </componentInstances>
        <componentInstances>
```

```
            <componentInstanceProperties>
                <name>entityNames</name>
                <value>Delivery__c,Return_Item__c</value>
            </componentInstanceProperties>
            <componentName>flexipage:recentItems</componentName>
        </componentInstances>
        <name>main</name>
    </flexiPageRegions>
    <masterLabel>Deliveries</masterLabel>
    <quickActionList>
        <quickActionListItems>
            <quickActionName>New_Delivery</quickActionName>
        </quickActionListItems>
    </quickActionList>
</FlexiPage>
```

The XML code is ready. Now it's time to deploy it, and the rest of the Deliveries package, into your organization.

Deploying a Flexible Page

As we mentioned at the start of this chapter, a Flexible Page has to be deployed via the Metadata API, and there are a few ways to do that: through the Force.com Migration Tool, the Force.com IDE, or Workbench.

You may have some of those already set up on your computer, but for the purposes of this exercise, we're going to choose the simplest route. We'll be deploying via the Workbench, which is an online suite of open-source tools designed for administrators and developers to interact with Salesforce organizations via the Force.com APIs.

Try It Out: Deploy a Flexible Page

We've created our Flexible Page XML, so now it's time to deploy it and its app into our developer organization.

1. Zip the contents of the `Salesforce1_Dev_Guide_Deliveries_App` package folder back up into a new `.zip` file called `DeliveriesApp.zip`.

    ![icon] **Important:** Don't zip up the main folder itself, or the package won't deploy correctly. Select the `package.xml` file and all the subfolders (objects, flexipages, tabs, and so on), and zip them up together.

2. In a new browser tab or window, navigate to https://developer.salesforce.com/page/Workbench.

3. Click **Login to Workbench Now on Developerforce**.

4. Set the API version to the latest one.

   For example, Summer '14 is API version 31.0. Flexible Pages are supported in API version 29.0 and later.

5. Agree to the terms of service, and then click **Login with Salesforce**.

6. Log in using your Developer Edition credentials.

7. From the migration menu, select Deploy.

8. Click **Choose File**, and then select the `DeliveriesApp.zip` file you just created that now contains our Flexible Page.

9. Select `Single Package`.

10. Click **Next**.

11. Click **Deploy**.

12. Wait for the deployment to finish.

13. Return to your Salesforce browser window.

Great! Now our package and its contents are in our development organization. But we're not done yet. We need to get our Flexible Page into Salesforce1, and to do that, we need to create a tab.

About Flexible Page Tabs

Before you can include a Flexible Page App Page in the Salesforce1 navigation menu, you must create a custom tab for it.

Flexible Page tabs don't work like other custom tabs in Salesforce. Once created, they don't show up on the All Tabs page when you click the plus icon (+) that appears to the right of your current tabs. Flexible Page tabs also don't show up in the Available Tabs list when you customize the tabs for your apps. Flexible Page tabs only facilitate inclusion of the Flexible Page in the Salesforce1 navigation menu.

You can define a Flexible Page tab in XML and deploy it like you would any other custom tab, but we're going to do it in the full Salesforce site to illustrate the Flexible Page tab's unique qualities.

Try It Out: Create a Flexible Page Tab

1. In Setup, go to **Create** > **Tabs**.

2. Click **New** in the Flexible Page Tabs related list.

The Flexible Page Tabs related list displays only if there is a Flexible Page deployed in your organization.

3. Select our Deliveries Flexible Page for the tab.

4. Enter *My Deliveries* as the label.

   This text becomes the name for the Flexible Page in the Salesforce1 navigation menu, and it also displays in the Flexible Page header along with its corresponding icon.

5. Click the `Tab Style` lookup icon to display the Tab Style Selector.

6. Click the **Globe** style.

   The icon on the style that you select is the icon that displays to the left of the Flexible Page label in the Salesforce1 navigation menu.

7. Click **Next**.

8. Leave the tab applied to all profiles.

   > Note: The Default On and Default Off options for Flexible Pages don't work as they do with other custom tabs. The Flexible Page menu item appears for the selected profiles in Salesforce1 whether you choose Default On or Default Off. Select the Tab Hidden option to hide the Flexible Page menu item from the selected profiles in Salesforce1.

9. Click **Save**.

   Example:

All right! The tab is created. Now we can make our Flexible Page available in Salesforce1.

Tell Me More: Flexible Page Tabs

Creating a Custom Tab Style

You can create your own custom tab style for your Flexible Page tab if your organization has access to the Documents tab. When in the tab style selector:

1. Click **Create your own style**.

2. Click the `Color` lookup icon to display the color selection dialog and click a color to select it.

3. Click **Insert an Image**, select the document folder, and select the image you want to use.

   Alternatively, click **Search in Documents**, enter a search term, and click **Go!** to find a document file name that includes your search term.

   > 📝 Note: This dialog only lists files in document folders that are under 20 KB and have the Externally Available checkbox selected in the document property settings. If the document used for the icon is later deleted, Salesforce replaces it with a default multicolor block icon (🧊).

4. Select a file and click **OK**. Then you're taken back to the New Custom Tab wizard.

Icon Guidelines

When creating a custom icon for use in a Flexible Page tab, follow the guidelines in Custom Icon Guidelines and Best Practices on page 62.

Making Your Flexible Page Available in Salesforce1

In Customizing the Salesforce1 Navigation Menu on page 25, we went over the Salesforce1 navigation menu items and some of the quirks about how navigation works. We also customized the navigation menu structure for the Acme Wireless mobile technicians. Later, in the Extending Salesforce1 with Visualforce Pages chapter on page 77, we added a Visualforce page to the menu.

Now it's time to augment the menu even further by adding our Flexible Page, and hence, our custom app, to the Salesforce1 navigation menu.

Try It Out: Add a Flexible Page to the Salesforce1 Navigation Menu

The first item you put in the menu becomes your users' Salesforce1 landing page. The Acme Wireless delivery drivers don't need to see the Deliveries app as their landing page every time they open Salesforce1, but they do need access to it. Let's put it in the Apps section of the menu.

1. From Setup, click **Salesforce1 Setup** > **Navigation Menu**.

2. In the list of available items, select our Flexible Page tab, My Deliveries, and click **Add**.

3. Using the **Up** and **Down** arrows, position My Deliveries just below the Smart Search Items menu item.

   This will make the Deliveries app the first item in the Apps section of the menu.

4. Click **Save**.

It's done! Let's go test it out in Salesforce1.

Test the Flexible Page in Salesforce1

1. Open the Salesforce1 app on your mobile device.

2. Tap ▤ to access the navigation menu.

3. Scroll down to the Apps section.

   This section contains any menu item that was put below the Smart Search Items element, whether it's really an "app" or not.

4. Tap **My Deliveries**.

   You're taken to the Flexible Page. The "My Deliveries" label is at the top, and we see two list cards representing Today's Deliveries and Recent Items. There aren't any deliveries in our developer organization, so the components are empty.

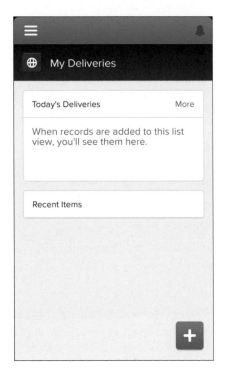

Example: The Today's Deliveries component picks up any delivery scheduled for today's date with a status of "In Transit". If we did have some records in our developer organization that matched those requirements, our Flexible Page might look like this:

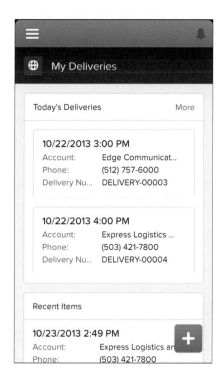

Tell Me More: Flexible Pages

When working with Flexible Pages, keep in mind that a Flexible Page region can contain no more than 25 components.

Modifying Flexible Pages

If you're considering making changes to a Flexible Page, some changes require an update to the XML, and others don't. You must modify the Flexible Page XML and re-deploy it if you change:

- Which list views are displayed
- The order that the different list views are displayed in (not the contents of the list view)
- The objects that show up in the recent items list
- The global actions that are available

Updates to these other items don't require a change to the Flexible Page XML, and can be done in the full Salesforce site.

- The contents of the list view components
- The global actions

Packaging Flexible Pages

For details on how Flexible Pages work in packages, see the *ISVforce Guide*.

CHAPTER 16 Development Guidelines and Best Practices

In this chapter ...

- When to Use the Navigation Menu or the Publisher
- Visualforce Guidelines and Best Practices
- Force.com Canvas Guidelines and Best Practices

You've had a chance to learn the major concepts of developing for the Salesforce1 app, and to see how you can easily add customized functionality for your mobile users. This chapter focuses on some conceptual guidelines and specific best practices for developing advanced custom actions and pages using the programmatic tools available to all Salesforce1 Platform developers.

Whether you're creating Visualforce pages to add as custom actions or mobile cards, or creating or integrating canvas apps into Salesforce1, these principles and practices will help you provide the best experience for your mobile users.

When to Use the Navigation Menu or the Publisher

As we've seen throughout the examples in this book, you can extend and customize the Salesforce1 app and make your new functionality accessible to users from either the navigation menu or from the publisher. Here we'll look at when you should use one method over another.

Navigation menu

The navigation menu appears when you tap ☰. This menu is available in the global context. For example, if users log in and are viewing items in the feed, they can tap and open the navigation menu, and it displays menu items. Typically, these menu items lead to more complex business processes that don't take place in the context of any particular object.

Menu items in the navigation menu should bring users to a fully functional page or app. So if you have a page or app that contains many fields through which the user would need to scroll and perform a more complex process, you'll want to make your page or app available from the navigation menu.

An example from this book is the Find Warehouses Visualforce page that we made available from the navigation menu in Extending Salesforce1 with Visualforce Pages on page 77. When the mobile technician taps the menu item, a page appears that contains a Google map and displays any nearby warehouses. The functionality of this page is global—not in the context of any particular object in our schema.

Publisher

The publisher appears when you tap 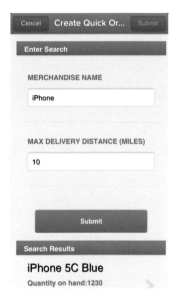. This menu is for accessing custom functionality that displays small amounts of data and allows users to perform short, quick actions. If you have functionality that occurs in the context of an object, you'll want to add it as an action in the publisher.

An example from this book is the Create Quick Order action available from the publisher within a customer account. While the mobile technicians are servicing a customer account, they can tap the action and then enter in just the merchandise name and distance to find warehouses with a part in stock. Then the technicians enter the quantity and a customer order is created. The functionality of this Visualforce page occurs within the context of a customer account. The user interaction with the page is quick, and it's a simple process to search and create an order because the page contains only a few fields.

Visualforce Guidelines and Best Practices

Visualforce pages aren't automatically mobile friendly in the Salesforce1 app. The standard Salesforce header and sidebar are disabled in favor of the Salesforce1 controls, and a JavaScript API is available to make it possible for Visualforce pages to connect with Salesforce1 navigation management. In other respects the pages remain as they are and, although usable within Salesforce1, desktop focused Visualforce pages will *feel* desktop focused.

Fortunately, making your apps look great in the Salesforce1 app is straightforward. You can either revise your code so that your pages work in both the full Salesforce site and the Salesforce1 app, or you can create mobile-specific pages.

In this chapter, you'll learn best practices for how to:

- Share Visualforce pages between mobile and desktop.
- Exclude Visualforce from mobile or desktop.
- Choose the best architecture for your Visualforce pages.
- Choose an effective page layout for your pages.
- Manage user input and navigation.
- Use Visualforce pages as custom actions.
- Tune your pages for the best performance.

Sharing Visualforce Pages Between Mobile and Desktop

You should revise Visualforce pages that appear in both the Salesforce1 app and in the full Salesforce site to support both environments. This includes Visualforce pages used as custom actions, and Visualforce pages added to standard page layouts, except those added to the Mobile Cards section of a page layout.

Visualforce pages that need to work in both environments include:

- Pages used as custom actions. Custom actions appear in the publisher in the Salesforce1 app, and in the publisher menu in the full Salesforce site.
- Pages added to normal page layouts, when `Available for Salesforce mobile apps` is enabled for the page.
- Custom Visualforce buttons or links added to normal page layouts.
- Standard button overrides with Visualforce pages for the New, Edit, View, Delete, and Clone actions. Overriding standard list and tab controls isn't supported in Salesforce1. Button overrides won't appear in the Salesforce1 app unless `Available for Salesforce mobile apps` is enabled for the page.

 Note: Standard buttons that are overridden with a Visualforce page disappear from record detail pages and record lists in Salesforce1 if `Available for Salesforce mobile apps` is disabled for the Visualforce page that overrides the corresponding button.

Excluding Visualforce Pages from Mobile or Desktop

To display your Visualforce pages only in the Salesforce1 app, add them to the Mobile Cards section of your page layout. To add Visualforce pages to either the Salesforce1 app or the full Salesforce site, use tab and navigation settings.

Visualforce pages that can be configured to be desktop-only or mobile-only include:

- Pages added as mobile cards on page layouts. These only appear in the Salesforce1 app.
- Pages added to normal page layouts, when `Available for Salesforce mobile apps` is disabled for the page. These only appear in the full Salesforce site.
- Pages used in Visualforce tabs. You add tabs to Salesforce1 navigation separately from adding them to the full Salesforce site navigation.

Choosing an Architecture for Visualforce Pages in Salesforce1

The Salesforce1 Platform supports several ways to design and structure Visualforce pages, each with different trade-offs with respect to development time, developer skill required, and how thoroughly you want your custom functionality to match Salesforce1.

Use one of the following approaches for the structure of your pages:

- Standard Visualforce Pages on page 173
- Mixed Visualforce and HTML on page 174
- JavaScript Remoting and Static HTML on page 177

Standard Visualforce Pages

Normal Visualforce pages render well on mobile browsers, and can be used as-is, with a modest reduction of the user experience compared to mobile-optimized Web pages. Pages display as they would on the full Salesforce site, and won't visually match other Salesforce1 features.

You saw how easy it is to add a Visualforce page to Salesforce1 in Extending Salesforce1 with Visualforce Pages on page 77.

Limitations

Limitations to the user experience include:

- Tap targets—buttons, links, form fields, and so on—are optimized for mouse cursors, and can be difficult to hit accurately with a fingertip.

- The visual design is unchanged, and may not fit with the mobile-optimized, modern visual design of Salesforce1.

If your development timeline is aggressive, you might find these limitations acceptable. Standard Visualforce development is documented in detail in the *Visualforce Developer's Guide*.

👁 Example: **Example of a Standard Visualforce Page**

The following code provides a sample for a standard Visualforce page that allows a user to edit a warehouse record. The edit feature is provided by the standard controller for the object.

```
<apex:page standardController="Warehouse__c">

<apex:form>

  <apex:pageBlock title="{! warehouse__c.Name }">

    <apex:pageBlockSection title="Warehouse Details" columns="1">

      <apex:inputField value="{! warehouse__c.Street_Address__c
}"/>
      <apex:inputField value="{! warehouse__c.City__c }"/>
      <apex:inputField value="{! warehouse__c.Phone__c }"/>
    </apex:pageBlockSection>

    <apex:pageBlockButtons location="bottom">
      <apex:commandButton action="{! quickSave }" value="Save"/>
    </apex:pageBlockButtons>

  </apex:pageBlock>

</apex:form>

</apex:page>
```

This page can be used in both the Salesforce1 app and the full Salesforce site. It displays as a standard desktop Visualforce page in both contexts.

Mixed Visualforce and HTML

Combine Visualforce tags for form elements and output text with static HTML for page structure to create mobile-friendly pages that more closely match the visual design of the Salesforce1 app. For mobile-only pages, you can quickly convert an existing Visualforce page, but this doesn't work as well for pages that are used in both the Salesforce1 app and the full Salesforce site.

Visualforce pages designed this way are still "standard" Visualforce, in that they use the standard request-response cycle, standard controller functionality, `<apex:inputField>` for form fields, POSTBACK and view state, and so on. The main difference from authoring pages for the full Salesforce site is the reduced or eliminated use of Visualforce tags to add structure to the page, in favor of static HTML. That is, replacing `<apex:pageBlock>`, `<apex:pageBlockSection>`, and so on, with `<div>`, `<p>`, `<span>`, and so on.

This approach also requires creating CSS stylesheets to manage the look-and-feel of the page elements, instead of using the built-in, automatically applied styles provided when you use the Visualforce components. While this can take some time, it allows you to much more closely match the visual design of Salesforce1. This also means that pages designed this way *won't* match the full Salesforce site visually.

Applying this Approach to Your Visualforce Pages

To use this approach for creating pages to use in Salesforce1, follow a few general rules.

- Don't use the following Visualforce tags:

    - `<apex:pageBlock>`
    - `<apex:pageBlockButtons>`
    - `<apex:pageBlockSection>`
    - `<apex:pageBlockSectionItem>`
    - `<apex:pageBlockTable>`

- Use `<apex:form>`, `<apex:inputField>` or `<apex:input>`, and `<apex:outputLabel>` for forms.
- Use `<apex:outputText>` or Visualforce for non-editable text.
- Use your preferred HTML to construct the structure for the page: `<div>`, `<span>`, `<h1>`, `<p>`, and so on.
- Use CSS styling to apply your preferred visual design.

Advantages and Limitations

The advantages of this approach include:

- Reasonably fast development time, and you use the normal Visualforce development tools and processes.
- It's reasonably easy to repurpose existing pages.
- You can more closely match the Salesforce1 look and feel.

Some limitations to keep in mind:

- This approach makes the usual Visualforce request round trips, with larger data payloads, compared to a fully mobile-optimized approach using JavaScript remoting.
- It's extra work to add CSS styles that replace the styles automatically added by `<apex:pageBlock>` and related components.

👁 Example: **Example of a Mixed Visualforce and HTML Page**

The following code sample shows a mixed HTML and Visualforce page that allows a user to edit a warehouse record. The edit feature is provided by the standard controller for the object.

```
<apex:page standardController="Warehouse__c">

<style>
    html, body, p { font-family: sans-serif; }
</style>

<apex:form >

    <h1>{!Warehouse__c.Name}</h1>

    <h2>Warehouse Details</h2>

    <div id="theForm">
        <div>
          <apex:outputLabel for="address" value="Street Address"/>

            <apex:inputField id="address"
                value="{! warehouse__c.Street_Address__c}"/>
        </div>
        <div>
            <apex:outputLabel for="city" value="City"/>
            <apex:inputField id="city"
                value="{! warehouse__c.City__c}"/>
        </div>
        <div>
            <apex:outputLabel for="phone" value="Phone"/>
            <apex:inputField id="phone"
                value="{! warehouse__c.Phone__c}"/>
        </div>
    </div>

    <div id="formControls">
        <apex:commandButton action="{!quickSave}" value="Save"/>
    </div>
```

```
</apex:form>

</apex:page>
```

This page can be used in both the Salesforce1 app and the full Salesforce site. It displays as a standard page on the full Salesforce site, but without the full Salesforce styling for the form. In the Salesforce1 app, it displays roughly matching the Salesforce1 visual style. With additional styles, the page can approximate the visual style for both versions.

JavaScript Remoting and Static HTML

Combine JavaScript remoting and static HTML to offer the best user experience, with the best performance and user interface match to Salesforce1. This architecture avoids most Visualforce tags in favor of rendering page elements in JavaScript. This option requires the most developer expertise, and can take a little longer to set up than standard Visualforce or mixed Visualforce and HTML. Use the Salesforce Mobile Packs for a fast start and to work with the very latest in mobile Web application technology.

Visualforce pages designed this way eschew many of the automatic, simplified features of standard Visualforce, in favor of taking more control over the request-response cycle, and performing page updates using JavaScript instead of page reloads. This can substantially improve the performance of the page, especially over the lower bandwidth, higher latency wireless network connections that make mobile devices so, well, mobile. The downside is that there is more code to write, and you need expertise in JavaScript, JavaScript remoting, HTML5, your mobile toolkit, and CSS, in addition to Apex and Visualforce. The upside of the downside is that you're working with the latest, most advanced tools for mobile development, and the pages you can build are the best, most complete way to "snap in" custom functionality that fully integrates with Salesforce1.

You can build desktop Visualforce pages using this approach as well as pages for Salesforce1. It's even possible to share such pages between the two environments by customizing the styling, though it's a challenge to closely match the full Salesforce site look and feel. Most importantly, the pages you design can be fully responsive, adapting and working across a range of devices and form factors.

Applying this Approach to Your Visualforce Pages

To use this approach for creating pages for the Salesforce1 app, follow this general process:

1. Install your preferred Salesforce Mobile Pack (available on Salesforce Developers) into your organization as a static resource.

2. Set your page's docType to `html-5.0`. Strongly consider disabling the standard stylesheets and header. For example:

```
<apex:page standardController="Warehouse__c"
    extensions="WarehouseEditor"
    showHeader="false" standardStylesheets="false"
    docType="html-5.0">
```

3. Add scripts and styles from your chosen mobile toolkit to the page using Visualforce resource tags. For example:

```
<apex:includeScript
    value="{!URLFOR(
        $Resource.Mobile_Design_Templates,
        'Mobile-Design-Templates-master/common/js/
            jQuery2.0.2.min.js'
    )}"/>
```

4. Use HTML5 and your mobile toolkit's tags and attributes to create a page skeleton.

5. Add JavaScript functions to the page as handlers to respond to user interaction. Use JavaScript remoting to call Apex `@RemoteAction` methods that retrieve records, perform DML, and so on.

6. Add additional JavaScript functions to handle user actions and page updates. Perform page updates by constructing HTML elements in JavaScript, and then adding or appending them to the page skeleton.

👁 Example: **Example of a JavaScript Remoting and Static HTML Page**

The following code sample shows a remoting + HTML Visualforce page that allows a user to edit a warehouse record. The edit feature is provided by a controller extension with `@RemoteAction` methods that respond to JavaScript remoting requests.

```
<apex:page standardController="Warehouse__c"
extensions="WarehouseEditor"
    showHeader="false" standardStylesheets="false"
    docType="html-5.0" applyHtmlTag="false" applyBodyTag="false">


    <!-- Include Mobile Toolkit styles and JavaScript -->
    <apex:stylesheet
      value="{!URLFOR($Resource.Mobile_Design_Templates,
      'Mobile-Design-Templates-master/common/css/app.min.css')}"/>
```

```
    <apex:includeScript
      value="{!URLFOR($Resource.Mobile_Design_Templates,

'Mobile-Design-Templates-master/common/js/jQuery2.0.2.min.js')}"/>

    <apex:includeScript
      value="{!URLFOR($Resource.Mobile_Design_Templates,

'Mobile-Design-Templates-master/common/js/jquery.touchwipe.min.js')}"/>

    <apex:includeScript
      value="{!URLFOR($Resource.Mobile_Design_Templates,
      'Mobile-Design-Templates-master/common/js/main.min.js')}"/>

<head>
<style>
    html, body, p { font-family: sans-serif; }
    input { display: block; }
</style>

<script>
    $(document).ready(function(){
        // Load the record
        loadWarehouse();
    });

    // Utility; parse out parameter by name from URL query string

    $.urlParam = function(name){
        var results = new RegExp('[\\?&]' + name + '=([^&#]*)')
            .exec(window.location.href);
        return results[1] || 0;
    }

    function loadWarehouse() {
        // Get the record Id from the GET query string
        warehouseId = $.urlParam('id');

        // Call the remote action to retrieve the record data
        Visualforce.remoting.Manager.invokeAction(
            '{!$RemoteAction.WarehouseEditor.getWarehouse}',
            warehouseId,
            function(result, event){;
```

```
                        if(event.status){
                            console.log(warehouseId);
                            $('#warehouse_name').text(result.Name);
                            $('#warehouse_address').val(
                               result.Street_Address__c);
                            $('#warehouse_city').val(result.City__c);
                            $('#warehouse_phone').val(result.Phone__c);
                        } else if (event.type === 'exception'){
                            console.log(result);
                        } else {
                            // unexpected problem...
                        }
                });
        }

        function updateWarehouse() {
            // Get the record Id from the GET query string
            warehouseId = $.urlParam('id');

            // Call the remote action to save the record data
            Visualforce.remoting.Manager.invokeAction(
                '{!$RemoteAction.WarehouseEditor.setWarehouse}',
                warehouseId, $('#warehouse_address').val(),
                    $('#warehouse_city').val(),
                    $('#warehouse_phone').val(),
                function(result, event){;
                        if(event.status){
                            console.log(warehouseId);
                            $('#action_status').text('Record updated.');
                        } else if (event.type === 'exception'){
                            console.log(result);
                            $('#action_status').text(
                               'Problem saving record.');
                        } else {
                            // unexpected problem...
                        }
                });
        }

</script>
</head>

<body>
```

```
<div id="detailPage">
    <div class="list-view-header" id="warehouse_name"></div>
    <div id="action_status"></div>

    <section>
        <div class="content">
            <h3>Warehouse Details</h3>
            <div class="form-control-group">
                <div class="form-control form-control-text">
                    <label for="warehouse_address">
                        Street Address</label>
                    <input type="text" id="warehouse_address" />
                </div>
                <div class="form-control form-control-text">
                    <label for="warehouse_city">City</label>
                    <input type="text" id="warehouse_city" />
                </div>
                <div class="form-control form-control-text">
                    <label for="warehouse_phone">Phone</label>
                    <input type="text" id="warehouse_phone" />
                </div>
            </div>
        </div>
    </section>

    <section class="data-capture-buttons one-buttons">
        <div class="content">
            <section class="data-capture-buttons one-buttons">
                <a href="#" id="updateWarehouse"
                    onClick="updateWarehouse();">save</a>
            </section>
        </div>
    </section>
</div> <!-- end detail page -->

</body>

</apex:page>
```

The static HTML provides the shell of the page, including empty form fields. JavaScript functions load the record, fill in the form fields, and send updated form data back to Salesforce.

Although this page can be used in the full Salesforce site, it's designed as a Salesforce1 app page and looks very different than a normal Visualforce page.

 Example: **Example of a JavaScript Remoting and Static HTML Controller**

Unlike the other two approaches to creating Salesforce1 pages, the remoting + HTML approach doesn't use standard controller functionality to retrieve data from and save data to Salesforce. Instead, you create a controller extension, or custom controller, to add any @RemoteAction methods your page requires. Here's a simplified controller extension that supports the above page.

```
global with sharing class WarehouseEditor {

    // Stub controller
    // We're only using RemoteActions, so this never runs
    public WarehouseEditor(ApexPages.StandardController ctl){ }

    @RemoteAction
    global static Warehouse__c getWarehouse(String warehouseId) {


        // Clean up the Id parameter, in case there are spaces
        warehouseId = warehouseId.trim();

        // Simple SOQL query to get the warehouse data we need
        Warehouse__c wh = [
            SELECT Id, Name, Street_Address__c, City__c, Phone__c

            FROM Warehouse__c
            WHERE Id = :warehouseId];

        return(wh);
    }

    @RemoteAction
    global static Boolean setWarehouse(
        String whId, String street, String city, String phone) {

        // Get the warehouse record for the Id
        Warehouse__c wh = WarehouseEditor.getWarehouse(whId);

        // Update fields
        // Note that we're not validating / sanitizing, for
simplicity
        wh.Street_Address__c = street.trim();
```

```
        wh.City__c = city.trim();
        wh.Phone__c = phone.trim();

        // Save the updated record
        // This should be wrapped in an exception handler
        update wh;

        return true;
    }
}
```

Visualforce Components to Avoid in Salesforce1

Most core Visualforce components (those components in the `apex` namespace) function normally within Salesforce1. Unfortunately, that doesn't mean they're optimized for mobile. You can improve the Salesforce1 user experience of your Visualforce pages by following some straightforward rules.

In general, avoid structural components, like `<apex:pageBlock>` and child components, and other components that mimic the Salesforce look and feel, such as `<apex:pageBlockTable>`. If you must use these components, set them to one column, using `<apex:pageBlockSection columns="1">`, instead of the default of two columns.

Avoid wide, non-wrapping components, especially `<apex:detail>`, `<apex:enhancedList>`, `<apex:listViews>`, and `<apex:relatedList>`, which are all unsupported. Keep device width in mind when creating tables with `<apex:dataTable>`.

Avoid using `<apex:inlineEditSupport>`. Inline editing is a user interface pattern that works well for mouse-based desktop apps, but it's difficult to use on a touch-based device, especially on phones where the screen is small.

Using `<apex:inputField>` is fine for fields that display as a basic input field, like text, email, and phone numbers, but avoid using it for field types that use an input widget, such as date and lookup fields.

Don't use `<apex:scontrol>`. sControls aren't supported anywhere in Salesforce1.

Unsupported Visualforce Components

Here's a list of Visualforce components that aren't supported in Salesforce1, and shouldn't be used in Visualforce pages that will be used with the Salesforce1 app.

- `<analytics:reportChart>`
- `<apex:detail>`

- `<apex:emailPublisher>`
- `<apex:enhancedList>`
- `<apex:flash>`
- `<apex:inputField>` for field types that use a widget for input, instead of a basic form field
- `<apex:listViews>`
- `<apex:logCallPublisher>`
- `<apex:relatedList>`
- `<apex:scontrol>`
- `<apex:sectionHeader>`
- `<apex:selectList>` for picklist fields
- `<apex:vote>`

> **Warning:** Embedded Visualforce pages—that is, those added to a page layout—that contain an `<apex:enhancedList>` component may cause the Salesforce1 app to crash on iOS.

Standard components outside the `apex` namespace, for example, `<liveagent:*>`, `<chatter:*>`, and so on, aren't supported in Salesforce1.

Custom components can be used in Visualforce in Salesforce1, as long as they themselves don't use unsupported components.

Choosing an Effective Page Layout

Design Visualforce pages that look good and work well within the Salesforce1 app by using a page layout appropriate for the context that the page is used in. Pages added as main navigation tabs or to the publisher can use nearly the full screen of the device, and can scroll vertically, while Visualforce added to an object's page layout has to fit within a specific, limited space.

In general, Visualforce added to page layouts works best if it's read-only, at-a-glance information. Put features that require user interaction, like multi-field forms, on full screen pages by adding them as tabs in the main navigation, or as custom actions from the publisher tray.

Mobile Card Layout

Mobile cards have the most limited layout, both in size and placement. Visualforce pages added as mobile cards on an object's page layout appear on the related lists page for the object in Salesforce1, as the first items on the page, below the header.

1. The record header displays when an record is loaded, but can be scrolled up and off the screen by the user. When on screen, it's 158 pixels high on all devices, and takes the full width of the screen. You can't control the display of the record header.

2. Mobile cards display above all of the related items on the record.

3. Set the width to 100%; the element sizes automatically, minus some padding on either side. The content of mobile cards can't be scrolled, so make sure it fits in the space you provide to it.

4. Control the height of the mobile card by setting the height in pixels in the page layout editor. The mobile card area uses exactly that height, even if the mobile card's content is shorter. In that case, the extra area is blank. If the card's content is taller, the content is clipped. As a best practice, don't create mobile cards taller than the smallest device screen you intend to support. Be sure to set the height of screen elements relevant to your environment.

5. The record's related items are displayed after all mobile cards.

While you can add multiple mobile cards, it quickly becomes a user experience challenge to scroll past them to the related lists. It's a best practice to add only one or two. If you need a full screen to display your page, consider moving it to a custom action on the object instead.

The normal Salesforce header and sidebar are automatically removed from Visualforce pages added as mobile cards. You may find it useful to explicitly turn them and the full Salesforce site stylesheets off while you're developing the page. Additionally, if your page uses the Google Maps API, Google recommends using an HTML5 doctype. Here's an `<apex:page>` tag that does all of these things:

```
<apex:page standardController="Warehouse__c"
    docType="html-5.0" showHeader="false" standardStylesheets="false">
```

Visualforce on a Page Layout

Visualforce pages added to an object's page layout display on the record details page. Unlike mobile cards, you can control the Visualforce element's placement on the Salesforce1 record details screen, putting fields and other record details above and below it, by changing its placement on the object's page layout. Visualforce pages added this way follow the same rules for ordering that fields and other elements do.

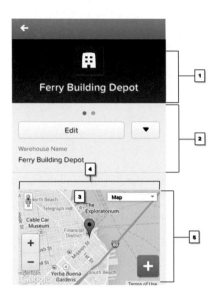

1. The record header displays when an record is loaded, but can be scrolled up and off the screen by the user. When on screen, it's 158 pixels high on all devices, and takes the full width of the screen. You can't control the display of the record header.

2. Record controls and details, automatically generated by Salesforce1.

3. A Visualforce page added to the object's page layout.

4. Set the width to 100%; the element sizes automatically, minus some padding on either side.

5. Control the height of the Visualforce page's area by setting the height of the item in pixels in the page layout editor. The Visualforce element uses exactly that height, even if the content is shorter. In that case, the extra area is blank. If the page's content is taller, the content is clipped. As a best practice, don't set inline Visualforce pages to be taller than the smallest device screen you intend to support.

As is the case with multiple cards, although you can add multiple inline Visualforce pages to a page layout, it quickly becomes a user experience challenge to scroll past them to see the rest of the page. It's a best practice to never add more than two Visualforce page elements in a row; separate Visualforce elements with a regular page element, such as a field. If you need a full screen to display your page, consider moving it to a custom action on the object instead.

Visualforce pages added to page layouts automatically have the normal Salesforce header and sidebar removed. You may find it useful to explicitly turn them and the full Salesforce site stylesheets off while you're developing the page. Additionally, if your page uses the Google Maps API, Google recommends using an HTML5 doctype. Here's an `<apex:page>` tag that does all of these things:

```
<apex:page standardController="Warehouse__c"
    docType="html-5.0" showHeader="false" standardStylesheets="false">
```

Full Screen Layout

Visualforce pages added to the Salesforce1 navigation menu, or as custom actions to the publisher tray, can use almost the entire screen, allowing more information, and more complex user interfaces.

1. The Salesforce1 header, which provides access to the main Salesforce1 menu, is 42 pixels high. The contents of the header can't be changed.

2. The rest of the device screen is dedicated to your Visualforce page.

When displayed in the Salesforce1 app, the standard Salesforce header and sidebar are automatically removed, like Visualforce pages used as mobile cards or added to page layouts. However, Visualforce pages used as custom actions in the publisher tray are shared with the full Salesforce site, and pages added to the Salesforce1 navigation may or may not be shared. Pages shared with the full Salesforce site shouldn't have the standard Salesforce header and sidebar explicitly removed unless removing the header and sidebar is the standard practice for all Visualforce on your site.

User Input and Interaction

Use `<apex:input>`, the `type` attribute, and pass-through HTML attributes to create mobile-friendly forms and user interfaces that are efficient and take advantage of native mobile browser features.

Without a keyboard and mouse, standard HTML forms can be difficult for users to fill out and interact with on mobile devices, especially phones. For Visualforce pages that don't use JavaScript remoting to make requests, choose Visualforce components for form input with an eye towards mobile users. No other change you can make to your Visualforce pages will have a larger usability impact than taking advantage of new HTML5 and mobile browser features to improve your forms and user interface controls.

Choose Efficient Input Elements

Use `<apex:input>` to get user input whenever possible. `<apex:input>` is an HTML5-ready, mobile-friendly, general-purpose input component that adapts to the data expected by a form field. It's even more flexible than `<apex:inputField>` because it uses the `type` attribute to allow client browsers to display type-appropriate user input widgets, such as a date picker, or use a type-specific keyboard that makes entering input on a mobile device much easier.

You can also use `<apex:inputField>` to create an HTML input element for a value that corresponds to a field on a Salesforce object. `<apex:inputField>` adapts the HTML generated to correspond with the data type of the underlying sObject field. Usually this is what you want, but if it isn't, use the `type` attribute to override the automatic data type detection. However, be aware that `<apex:inputField>` generates a lot of HTML, and requires additional resources to load, which means it's not the most efficient component to use over a mobile wireless connection.

Use the `type` Attribute to Create Mobile-Friendly Input Elements

Set the `type` attribute on `<apex:input>` components—and `<apex:inputField>`, if you're using it—to display data-type-specific keyboards and other input user interface widgets that are easier to use on touchscreens. The value is passed through to the generated HTML `<input>` element, for display in the Salesforce1 app.

As users step through form elements, the input method for that form element adapts for the type of data expected. Text fields show the standard keyboard, email fields show an email-specific keyboard with characters like the "@" sign and ".com" assigned to keys, date fields show a date picker, and so on.

Here's an example of a form that illustrates how this works:

```
<apex:form >

    <apex:outputLabel value="Phone" for="phone"/>
    <apex:input id="phone" value="{!fPhone}" type="tel"/><br/>

    <apex:outputLabel value="Email" for="email"/>
    <apex:input id="email" value="{!fText}" type="email"/><br/>

    <apex:outputLabel value="That Number" for="num"/>
    <apex:input id="num" value="{!fNumber}" type="number"/><br/>

    <apex:outputLabel value="The Big Day" for="date"/>
    <apex:input id="date" value="{!fDate}" type="date"/><br/>

</apex:form>
```

As the user moves through the form fields, either by tapping into them or tapping the **Next** button, the keyboard changes to match the expected data for the field.

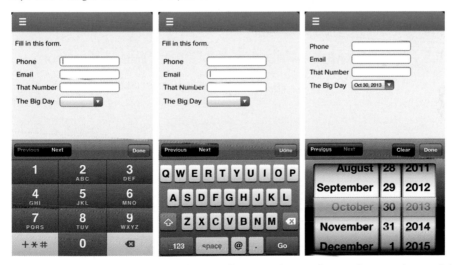

These type-specific keyboards make filling in forms much easier for people using their mobile devices on the go.

`<apex:input>` allows the following explicit `type` values to be set:

- date
- datetime
- datetime-local

- month
- week
- time
- email
- number
- range
- search
- tel
- text
- url

You can also set `type` to auto, and the data type of the associated controller property or method is used.

The HTML `type` attribute, including new HTML5 features, is a standard part of HTML. For additional details about the `type` attribute, what you can use it for, and how it relates to mobile development, see WHATWG's list of input `type` attribute values and descriptions. Not all values are supported on Visualforce input components. If you want to use a value not supported by Visualforce, use static HTML instead of a Visualforce tag.

Use HTML5 Pass-Through Attributes for Client-Side Validation

Set pass-through attributes on your `<apex:input>` and other Visualforce components to enable other HTML5 features, such as client-side validation. By performing basic validation on the client side, you can avoid sending a request to the server and waiting for a response, when there are easily-corrected errors on a form.

Attributes prefixed with `html-` are passed through to the generated HTML, with the prefix removed. To enable client-side validation, set an `html-pattern` attribute on the `<apex:input>` tag to match expected form values. This will add a `pattern` attribute to the generated `<input>` tag, enabling client-side validation for that field.

 Note: Client-side validation requires that the Visualforce page be set to API version 29.0 or later, and the page `docType` be set to `html-5.0`.

Validation patterns are regular expressions. Form input is checked against the expression, and if it matches, the field input is considered valid. If it doesn't match, the input is considered invalid; an error message is displayed, and the form won't be submitted to the server. Here's an example of a field that requires an email address from a specific domain:

```
<apex:input id="email" value="{!fText}" type="email"
    html-placeholder="you@example.com"
```

```
html-pattern="^[a-zA-Z0-9._-]+@example.com$"
title="Please enter an example.com email address"/>
```

Other useful HTML5 attributes that can be set as pass-through attributes include:

- `placeholder` (set using the `html-placeholder` attribute)—adds ghost text to the field to show sample input to the user.

- `title` (set using the `title` attribute on `<apex:input>`, and the `html-title` attribute on components without a title attribute)—adds an error message to use if the field fails client-side validation.

For inspiration for how you can use attributes to enhance the usability of HTML `<input>` elements, HTML5 Forms Introduction and New Attributes is a good survey of the new features in HTML5. For further details, especially for mobile users, and details of client-side forms validation, see Client-side form validation and Improving the user experience on mobile devices in WHATWG's HTML: The Living Standard.

Managing Navigation

Salesforce1 manages navigation using events. The navigation event framework is made available as a JavaScript object that provides a number of utility functions that make creating programmatic navigation that "just works" a breeze. The advantage is a navigation experience that's more natural for a mobile context. It also makes creating post-completion navigation, such as redirecting to an order page after the order is successfully submitted, easier for Salesforce1 developers.

In Salesforce1, programmatic navigation for Visualforce pages generally works something like this:

1. A user invokes a Visualforce page, usually from the navigation menu, or from the publisher.

2. The Visualforce page loads and runs, including any custom controller or extension code called by the page.

3. The user interacts with the page in some way: for example, to fill in some form values.

4. The user submits the form, or performs some other action on the page that commits a change.

5. Controller or extension code runs, saving the changes to Salesforce, and returning the results of the action.

6. The Visualforce page, using JavaScript response handlers, receives the results of the action, and when successful, responds by redirecting the user to a new page that shows the results of their action.

This scenario is easily handled by the Salesforce1 navigation framework.

Another common use case is simply adding links or other user interface controls to a page, which move from that Visualforce page to another page in Salesforce1. This navigation is also easily managed by the Salesforce1 navigation framework.

In these cases, navigation is handled by a special utility JavaScript object, `sforce.one`. The `sforce.one` object is automatically added to all Visualforce pages when they run inside the Salesforce1 app. This object provides a number of functions that trigger navigation events when they run. To use these functions, you can call them directly from your page's JavaScript code, or you can attach calls as click handlers to elements on the page.

Here's a JavaScript function, from the **FindNearbyWarehousesPage** page introduced in Extending Salesforce1 with Visualforce Pages on page 77, which creates markers to add to a Google map.

```
function setupMarker(){

    // Use JavaScript nav function to determine if we are
    // in Salesforce1 and set navigation link appropriately
    var warehouseNavUrl =
        'sforce.one.navigateToSObject(\'' + warehouse.Id + '\')';

    // Wrap the warehouse details with the link to
    // navigate to the warehouse details
    var warehouseDetails =
        '<a href="javascript:' + warehouseNavUrl + '">' +
        warehouse.Name + '</a><br/>' +
        warehouse.Street_Address__c + '<br/>' +
        warehouse.City__c + '<br/>' +
        warehouse.Phone__c;

    // Create a panel that will appear when a marker is clicked
    var infowindow = new google.maps.InfoWindow({
        content: warehouseDetails
    });

    // ...
}
```

The very first line builds a string, *warehouseNavUrl*, that, when used as a JavaScript URL, navigates to the detail page for the warehouse. The link is created around the warehouse name, and appears in the information panel (put together in the *warehouseDetails* string) that appears when you click a marker. Clicking the warehouse name takes you to the detail page for that warehouse (the omitted part of the function code deals with the Google Maps API calls to create a marker and add it to the map).

If you have JavaScript code or HTML markup that runs inside of Salesforce1, keep these considerations in mind:

- Don't directly manipulate the browser URL using `window.location.href`. This doesn't work well with the Salesforce1 navigation management system.

- Don't use `target="_blank"` in navigation URLs; you can't open new windows inside Salesforce1.

Navigation Methods within the Force.com Canvas Framework

If you're using Force.com Canvas, there's a simpler way to control navigation around canvas apps and canvas personal apps in Salesforce1.

You can use Force.com methods to control navigation in Salesforce1. These methods within the Force.com Canvas framework are events that reside in the JavaScript library. When you call one of the navigation methods from your canvas code, you send an event into Salesforce1 that reads the payload and directs the user to the specified destination.

Reference the navigation method as an event variable, with name and payload. For example:

```
var event = {name:"s1.createRecord", payload: {entityName: "Account",
recordTypeId: "00h300000001234"}};
```

For more information about using the new methods, see "Salesforce1 Navigation Methods for Use with Canvas Apps" in the Force.com Canvas Developer's Guide.

Navigation with the `sforce.one` Object

The Salesforce1 Platform includes an event mechanism for navigation. This is exposed in Visualforce as a JavaScript object called `sforce.one`. It's available in any page that appears in Salesforce1.

The `sforce.one` object provides the following functions. Reference the function using dotted notation from the `sforce.one` object. For example: `sforce.one.navigateToSObject(recordId, view)`.

Function	Description
`back([refresh])`	Navigates to the previous state that's saved in the `sforce.one` history. It's equivalent to clicking a browser's Back button.
	`refresh` is optional. By default, the page doesn't refresh. Pass `true` to refresh the page if possible.
`navigateToSObject(recordId[, view])`	Navigates to an sObject record, specified by `recordId`. This record "home" has several views, which in Salesforce1 are available as slides that the user can swipe between.
	`view` is optional and defaults to `detail`. `view` specifies the slide within record home to display initially. The possible values are as follows.
	• `detail`: the record detail slide

Function	Description
	• `chatter`: the Chatter slide
	• `related`: the view of related slide
`navigateToURL(url[, isredirect])`	Navigates to the specified URL.
	Relative and absolute URLs are supported. Relative URLs are relative to the one.app domain, and retain navigation history. External URLs—that is, URLs that are outside the Salesforce1 app—open in a separate browser window.
	Use relative URLs to navigate to different screens within your app. Use external URLs to allow the user to access a different site or app, where they can take actions that don't need to be preserved in your app. To return to your app, the separate window that's opened by an external URL must be closed when the user is finished with the other app. The new window has a separate history from your app, and this history is discarded when the window is closed. This also means that the user can't click a Back button to go back to your app; the user must close the new window.
	`mailto:`, `tel:`, `geo:`, and other URL schemes are supported for launching external apps and attempt to "do the right thing." However, support varies by mobile platform and device. `mailto:` and `tel:` are reliable, but we recommend that you test any other URLs on a range of expected devices.
	📝 Note: Only standard URL schemes are supported by `navigateToURL`. To access custom schemes, use `window.location` instead.
	`isredirect` is optional and defaults to `false`. Set it to `true` to indicate that the new URL should replace the current one in the navigation history.
`navigateToFeed( subjectId, type)`	Navigates to the feed of the specified `type`, scoped to the `subjectId`. For some feed `type`s, the `subjectId` is required but ignored. For those feed `type`s, pass the current user's ID as the `subjectId`.
	`type` is the feed type. The possible values are as follows.

Function	Description
	• `BOOKMARKS`: Contains all feed items saved as bookmarks by the context user. Pass the current user's ID as the `subjectId`.
	• `COMPANY`: Contains all feed items except feed items of type `TrackedChange`. To see the feed item, the user must have sharing access to its parent. Pass the current user's ID as the `subjectId`.
	• `FILES`: Contains all feed items that contain files posted by people or groups that the context user follows. Pass the current user's ID as the `subjectId`.
	• `GROUPS`: Contains all feed items from all groups the context user either owns or is a member of. Pass the current user's ID as the `subjectId`.
	• `NEWS`: Contains all updates for people the context user follows, groups the user is a member of, files and records the user is following, all updates for records whose parent is the context user, and every feed item and comment that mentions the context user or that mentions a group the context user is a member of. Pass the current user's ID as the `subjectId`.
	• `PEOPLE`: Contains all feed items posted by all people the context user follows. Pass the current user's ID as the `subjectId`.
	• `RECORD`: Contains all feed items whose parent is a specified record, which could be a group, user, object, file, or any other standard or custom object. When the record is a group, the feed also contains feed items that mention the group. When the record is a user, the feed contains only feed items on that user. Pass the record's ID as the `subjectId`.
	• `TO`: Contains all feed items with mentions of the context user, feed items the context user commented on, and feed items created by the context user that are commented on. Pass the current user's ID as the `subjectId`.
	• `TOPICS`: Contains all feed items that include the specified topic. Pass the topic's ID as the `subjectId`.
`navigateToFeedItemDetail( feedItemId)`	Navigates to the specific feed item, `feedItemId`, and any associated comments.

Function	Description
`navigateToRelatedList(` `relatedListId,` `parentRecordId)`	Navigates to a related list for the `parentRecordId`. For example, to display a related list for a Warehouse object, the `parentRecordId` is `Warehouse__c.Id`.
	`relatedListId` is the API name or ID of the related list to display.
`navigateToList(` `listViewId,` `listViewName, scope)`	Navigates to the list view that's specified by the `listViewId`, which is the ID of the list view to be displayed.
	`listViewName` sets the title for the list view. It doesn't need to match the actual name that's saved for the list view. To use the saved name, set `listViewName` to null.
	Set `scope` to the name of the sObject in the view, for example, "Account" or "MyObject__c".
`createRecord(` `entityName[,` `recordTypeId])`	Opens the page to create a new record for the specified `entityName`, for example, "Account" or "MyObject__c".
	`recordTypeId` is optional and, if provided, specifies the record type for the created object.
`editRecord(recordId)`	Opens the page to edit the record specified by `recordId`.

Keep the following in mind when using the `sforce.one` object:

- Calls to `sforce.one.navigateToURL` may result in an "Unsupported Page" error if the URL references standard pages for objects or Chatter pages. To avoid this error, ensure that the URL begins with a backslash (`/_ui` instead of `_ui`).
- The `sforce.one.createRecord` method doesn't respect Visualforce overrides on the standard action.

How `sforce.one` Handles API Versions

The `sforce.one` object is frequently improved in new releases of the Salesforce1 Platform. To maintain backward compatibility, `sforce.one` provides version-specific behavior, and you can use a specific version of `sforce.one` in your apps.

By default, `sforce.one` uses the same version as the API version of the requested Visualforce page. For example, if a Visualforce page has an API version of 30.0, JavaScript on that page that uses `sforce.one` by default uses the API version 30.0 of `sforce.one`.

This means that when a Visualforce page is updated to a new API version, the page automatically uses the updated version of `sforce.one`. In the preceding example, if that Visualforce page is updated to API version 31.0, app functionality that uses `sforce.one` uses the API version 31.0 of `sforce.one`.

If updated behavior in a new API version of `sforce.one` causes compatibility problems with the page's features, you have three options for correcting the problem.

- Revert the Visualforce page's API version to the prior version. This action requires no code changes.
- Update the code for the page's features to fix the problem. This solution is best, but it might require some debugging, and it will definitely require code changes.
- Use a specific version of `sforce.one`. This solution often requires minimal code changes.

 Note: `sforce.one` was added in Winter '14 (API version 29.0) and wasn't versioned until Summer '14 (API version 31.0). All versions of `sforce.one` earlier than version 31.0 are identical to version 31.0. You can specify a version of `sforce.one` for any version that's valid for Visualforce, that is, from version 15.0 to the current API version.

Using a Specific Version of `sforce.one`

To use a specific version of `sforce.one`, use the `sforce.one.getVersion()` function and provide it with the API version and a callback function that needs to use a specific version of `sforce.one`. The appropriate versions of `sforce.one` are automatically loaded by this call.

The signature for `sforce.one.getVersion()` is:

```
sforce.one.getVersion(versionString, callbackFunction);
```

`versionString` is the API version that your application requires. It's always two digits, a period, and one digit, such as "30.0". Calls with invalid version strings fail silently.

`callbackFunction` is a JavaScript function that uses a specific version of `sforce.one`. `sforce.one.getVersion()` operates asynchronously, and your callback function is called when it finishes loading the requested version of `sforce.one`. Your callback function receives a single parameter, an `sforce.one` object for the specified API version. Use the object passed in instead of the global `sforce.one` to make calls to `sforce.one` that conform to the API version that your app requires.

Examples of Using a Specific Version of `sforce.one`

The next examples all add a Create Account function to the following input button:

```
<input type="button" value="Create Account" onclick="btnCreateAccount()"
  id="btnCreateAcct"/>
```

Defaulting to the Visualforce Page's API Version

App code that should use the default version of `sforce.one`—the version that corresponds to the Visualforce Page's API version—doesn't need to ask for a version. Using that version happens automatically, and the code is straightforward.

```
<script>
    function MyApp() {
        this.createAccount = function() {
            sforce.one.navigateToURL("/001/e");
        };
    }

    var app = new MyApp();

    function btnCreateAccount() {
        app.createAccount();
    }
</script>
```

App functionality is created in a `MyApp` object, and then an event handling function calls the app function when that event, a button click, occurs. Separating application functionality from application event handling is a best practice, and it sets you up for using version-specific versions of `sforce.one`.

Using a Specific `sforce.one` API Version (Simple)

To use a specific version of `sforce.one`, get and save a reference to a versioned instance of the object. Then use this object to make `sforce.one` calls. The simplest way is to save it in the `MyApp` object. In the next sample, references to the versioned instance of `sforce.one` are in bold.

```
<script>
    function MyApp(sfone) {
        this.createAccount = function() {
            sfone.navigateToURL("/001/e");
        };
    }

    var app30 = null;
```

```
    function btnCreateAccount() {
        // Create our app object if not already defined
        if(!app30) {
            // Create app object with versioned sforce.one
            sforce.one.getVersion("30.0", function(sfoneV30) {
                app30 = new MyApp(sfoneV30);
                app30.createAccount();
            });
            return;
        }
        app30.createAccount();
    }
</script>
```

In the preceding example, the event-handling function is expanded from the first example to include the creation of a version-specific instance of `sforce.one`. If your app needs to mix multiple versions, you can create multiple `MyApp` instances with appropriate versions and names. More than one or two, though, are cumbersome to manage. We recommend the next approach instead.

Using a Specific `sforce.one` API Version (Best)

A better way to organize your app code is to create version-specific instances of `sforce.one` in an app initialization block of code so you can keep the event handling separate.

```
<script>
    function MyApp(sfone) {
        this.createAccount = function() {
            sfone.navigateToURL("/001/e");
        };
    }

    var app30 = null;

    // Initialize app: get versioned API, wire up clicks
    sforce.one.getVersion("30.0", function(sfoneV30) {
        // Create app object with versioned sforce.one
        app30 = new MyApp(sfoneV30);

        // Wire up button event
        var btn = document.getElementById("btnCreateAcct");
        btn.onclick = btnCreateAccount;
    });

    // Events handling functions
```

```
    // Can't be fired until app is defined
    function btnCreateAccount() {
        app30.createAccount();
    }
</script>
```

In this sample the app initialization is separated only by white space and comments, but you can separate it into functions for better encapsulation.

Using a Specific `sforce.one` API Version (Synchronous)

You can trigger a synchronous mode for `sforce.one` by manually including the specific version of `sforce.one`'s JavaScript on your page. The format for the URL to the library is: `/sforce/one/`*sforceOneVersion*`/api.js`. Here's an example:

```
<script src="/sforce/one/30.0/api.js"></script>
<script>
    function MyApp(sfone) {
        this.createAccount = function() {
            sfone.navigateToURL("/001/e");
        };
    }

    var app = null;

    sforce.one.getVersion("30.0", function(sfoneV30) {
        app = new MyApp(sfoneV30);
    });

    // Events handling function
    // Can't be fired until app is defined
    function btnCreateAccount() {
        app.createAccount();
    }
</script>
```

Although some situations require synchronous mode, the asynchronous version is preferred. If you forget to manually include the correct versions of the `sforce.one` library, your code will contain bugs that are difficult to diagnose.

Visual Design Considerations

Create Visualforce pages that more closely match the look of Salesforce1 by using CSS styling, responsive design, and minimal HTML.

Fonts and Styles

The visual design for Salesforce1 uses Proxima Nova, a sans-serif typeface licensed specially for Salesforce1. People in your organization might not have the font installed on their devices, but the following CSS fonts will use the closest matching font available:

```
p {
    font-family: "ProximaNovaSoft-Regular", Calibri,
        "Gill Sans", "Gill Sans MT", Candara, Segoe, "Segoe UI",
        Arial, sans-serif;
}
```

Change the selectors to match the appropriate text blocks and styles on your pages.

You might also consider slightly increasing the size of the font used for normal text and form elements. This makes them easier to read and, for form elements, to tap into. Here's a complete style block to get you started:

```
<style>
    html, body, p {
        font-family: "ProximaNovaSoft-Regular", Calibri,
            "Gill Sans", "Gill Sans MT", Candara, Segoe,
            "Segoe UI", Arial, sans-serif;
        font-size: 110%;
    }
    input { font-size: 95%; }
</style>
```

 Warning: Directly referencing Salesforce1 style sheets in your pages, or depending on styles found in them, isn't supported. As Salesforce1 evolves, the styles will change in ways that you won't expect. Pages that depend on unsupported styles may eventually break.

HTML Markup

If your organization's Visualforce pages match the full Salesforce site's look and feel, it's probably by using the Salesforce header, sidebar, styling, and `<apex:pageBlock>` and child components. Don't explicitly disable these elements, by setting `<apex:page showHeader="false" standardStylesheets="false" ...>`; Salesforce1 automatically disables these elements when the page runs inside it.

However, you may want to reconsider using `<apex:pageBlock>` and child components, because they explicitly match the full Salesforce site look and feel, and even with standard stylesheets turned off, the markup they generate carries over into Salesforce1. This makes your markup more complex, and it's harder to apply styling that matches Salesforce1.

Instead, use simple, static HTML markup, or the markup required by your chosen Mobile Toolkit. Sample markup is included the next section.

Responsive Design

Salesforce1 pages use responsive design techniques to provide device-optimized layouts, a stacked single column layout for phones, and a side-by-side, two-column layout for tablets. You can use a similar technique for your Visualforce pages used in Salesforce1.

First, your page should establish a default layout:

```css
/* Default CSS: 2 columns */
.content-block {
    width: 50%;
    float: left;
}
```

Second, use CSS styling and media queries to make the layout responsive:

```css
/* CSS phone */
@media screen and (max-width: 767px) {
    .content-block {
        width: 100%;
        float: none;
    }
}
```

Try it yourself in a Visualforce page using this HTML. Place the above CSS snippets between `<style>` tags on the same Visualforce page as the HTML, and then drag the corners of your browser window to observe the responsive layout.

```html
<!-- HTML for two blocks of content -->
<!-- On a phone they live underneath each other -->
<!-- On bigger screens they live next to each other -->

<div class="content-block">
    top on the phone, left on big screens
</div>

<div class="content-block">
    bottom on the phone, right on big screens
</div>
```

Using Visualforce Pages as Custom Actions

If your Visualforce page is used as a custom action, design it so that it either acts upon a single record provided by a standard controller, or finds and acts upon a record, or records your custom controller code retrieves.

Custom Actions on an Object

Visualforce pages added as custom actions on an object are invoked in the context of a record of that object type. That is to say, the custom action has a specific record ID handed to it, the record the user was looking at when they clicked the custom action, and the page should be designed to act upon that specific record type.

Visualforce pages used as custom actions on an object must use the standard controller for that object. Use controller extensions to add custom code, including `@RemoteAction` methods you can call using JavaScript remoting.

Your custom code may very well do more than make updates to the originating record. For example, the Create Quick Order custom action searches for matching merchandise, and creates an invoice and line item, all as part of creating an order for a part. That logic occurs in the context of the originating account record—the invoice is associated to the account record where the quick order action was invoked.

As a general rule, when the action completes, the user should be redirected to a page related to the originating record.

Custom Global Actions

Visualforce pages used as global actions can be invoked in many different places, and don't have a specific record associated with them. They have complete "freedom of action," which means it's up to you to write the code.

More specifically, Visualforce pages used as global actions can't use *any* standard controller. You must write a custom controller to handle the page. Your code might create one or many records, modify found records, and so on.

When a global action completes, the user should usually be either redirected to a parent record created as part of the action, or returned to where they started.

Creating Visualforce Pages That Work in Mobile and Desktop

Create Visualforce pages that work well in both the Salesforce1 app and the full Salesforce site by writing code that adapts to the context it's running in.

As you learned in Managing Navigation on page 191, Salesforce1 provides a framework for handling various navigation controls and events. That framework isn't available to Visualforce pages when they run on the full Salesforce site, because the `sforce` object is injected onto pages only inside Salesforce1. This means that, for pages shared between the Salesforce1 app and the full Salesforce site, you'll want to write code that uses the `sforce` object when it's available, and standard Visualforce navigation when it's not.

For example, here is a bit of JavaScript that runs after a JavaScript remoting request successfully returns from the `@RemoteAction` method that creates a quick order. This code is from a Visualforce page that's used as a custom action, which adds it to the publisher in the Salesforce1 app and the publisher menu in the full Salesforce site. It needs to work in both places. The intent of the code is to navigate to the detail page for the account for whom the order was placed:

```
// Go back to the Account detail page
if( (typeof sforce != 'undefined') && (sforce != null) ) {
    // Salesforce1 navigation
    sforce.one.navigateToSObject(aId);
}
else {
    // Set the window's URL using a Visualforce expression
    window.location.href =
        '{!URLFOR($Action.Account.View, account.Id)}';
}
```

The `if` statement checks to see if the `sforce` object is available and usable. This is only true if the page is running inside Salesforce1. If `sforce` is available, the Salesforce1 navigation management system is used to go to the account's detail page.

If the `sforce` object isn't available, trying to use it to navigate anywhere results in a JavaScript error, and no navigation. So, instead, the code sets the window's URL using a Visualforce expression that returns the URL for the account's detail page. You don't want to do this in Salesforce1 because the navigation event will be lost by the framework, but it's required in normal Visualforce.

For more details on how to use the `$Action` global variable to create URLs for different kinds of objects and actions, see the Global Variables appendix in the *Visualforce Developer's Guide*.

Performance Tuning for Visualforce Pages

Performance is an important aspect of mobile Visualforce pages. Visualforce has a caching mechanism to help you tune the performance of your pages.

To enable caching for a page, use this statement:

```
<apex:page cache="true" expires="600">
```

The parameters for page caching are:

Attribute	Description
cache	Boolean value that specifies whether the browser should cache the page. If not specified, defaults to `false`.
expires	Integer value that specifies the period of cache in seconds.

For more information, see Force.com Sites Best Practices on Developerforce

More Resources

Here are some more resources to help you tune the performance of your Salesforce1 apps:

- Inside the Force.com Query Optimizer (webinar)
- Maximizing the Performance of Force.com SOQL, Reports, and List Views (blog post)
- Force.com SOQL Best Practices: Nulls and Formula Fields (blog post)

Force.com Canvas Guidelines and Best Practices

There are some additional best practices and guidelines to keep in mind when exposing your applications as canvas apps and making them available to mobile users.

Force.com Canvas makes it easy for you to integrate Web applications with Salesforce1 at the user interface level. However, the user experience in the Salesforce1 app is different than in the full Salesforce site. You'll want to make sure you design your canvas apps for mobile users and be sure to test them in the mobile environment.

Canvas Apps in the Publisher

Keep these best practices and guidelines in mind when making your canvas apps available in the publisher.

- When you access a canvas app from the publisher in the full Salesforce site, the user interface is different than when you access a canvas app from the publisher in the Salesforce1 app. For example, in the feed in the full Salesforce site, the Share button is at the bottom of the feed item.

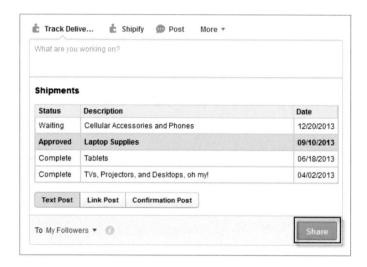

In the Salesforce1 app, the Share button is at the top of the screen.

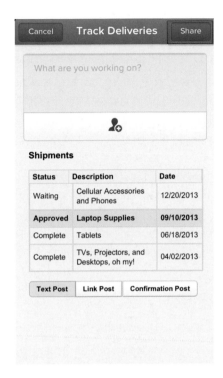

- When creating a canvas custom action, the height available for that action in the full Salesforce site is much greater than the height for that action in Salesforce1. Use the Dimensions object in the Force.com Canvas SDK to render your canvas app in the correct size.

- Keep the labels for canvas custom actions concise. Longer labels may not fully display in the publisher.

- When you access a canvas app from the publisher, the *What are you working on?* pane appears above the canvas app. This pane remains fixed, even if your canvas app scrolls.

- When the request comes into your Web application that's exposed as a canvas app, you can determine the type of device that's making the request. Use this information to render your app based on the requesting device for a better user experience. For example, you can add logic so that if the request comes from a mobile phone, only four lines of text are displayed; if the request comes from a tablet, ten lines of text are displayed.

- In most cases, you'll want to specify 100% for the canvas app height and width in your CSS. This ensures that the canvas app takes up the maximum available screen space.

- Canvas apps appear in an iFrame, so you can format the app appearance as you would any standard iFrame.

Canvas Apps in the Feed

Keep these best practices and guidelines in mind when making your canvas apps available in the feed.

- On a mobile device, the link text and description for a feed item display fewer characters than in the full Salesforce site. Keep this in mind when programmatically creating feed items.

- When a canvas app is contained in a feed item, the feed item appears with a link to the canvas app. On a mobile device, the canvas app doesn't appear in the feed; instead, a new page opens and displays the canvas app.

- In the Salesforce1 mobile browser app, the screen changes if the device is rotated. Your canvas app should support rotation, if possible, to maintain a seamless user experience. Note that the Salesforce1 downloadable app doesn't rotate.

- If your canvas app appears as a feed item, keep in mind that it will display in the feed on a mobile device so you'll want to render a mobile-friendly user interface.

Canvas Apps Context

When you display a canvas app inside the Salesforce1 app, keep these considerations in mind.

When you display a canvas app inside of the feed or publisher, the canvas context you receive (either from the signed request or from the `getContext` call) contains information specific to the Salesforce1 publisher.

- You can verify you're on either the feed or publisher by looking at the `displayLocation` value in the environment section. For publisher, `displayLocation` is set to **_Publisher_**. For the feed, `displayLocation` is set to **_ChatterFeed_**.

- When creating a canvas feed item, you can specify a `JSON` string as the parameter's value. When the context is sent, any value in the parameter's field on the feed item is sent in the parameters of the environment section of the context.

- As with any canvas app, the context contains information about the app dimensions. Since Salesforce1 is designed for mobile, the sizes we provide are different than for the full Salesforce site.

- For a single-finger touch scrolling experience:

  - Ensure that the outermost `div` elements contain the following properties:

    - min-height: 250px;
    - overflow: scroll;
    - width: 100%;
    - -webkit-overflow-scrolling: touch;
    - -webkit-transform: translated(0%,0px,0px);

- Set the `height` attribute to the `clientHeight` value delivered in the signed request. For example:

```
//Where sr is a parsed signed request object
var h = parseInt(sr.context.environment.
    dimensions.clientHeight, 10);
Sfdc.canvas.byId('divElementId').style.height = h;
```

- The `clientHeight` value can be very small, particularly in a phone's landscape mode, and users may not be able to see any content. Use `min-height` set to the desired height in pixels to ensure a good user experience.

Custom Icons for Canvas Apps

Keep these best practices and guidelines in mind when you add custom icons to your canvas apps.

You can customize the icon that is used in the Salesforce1 navigation menu. You set this icon in the Icon URL entry in the Basic Information section of the connected app settings for your canvas app. From Setup, click **Create** > **Apps** and click **Edit** for your connected app. The icon URL must be a secure HTTPS URL that points to an icon image file. The image file must be in the GIF, JPG, or PNG file format. For the Salesforce1 navigation menu, the icon cannot be larger than 60 pixels high by 60 pixels wide.

The custom icon that is used in the Salesforce1 navigation menu is also used in the Chatter tab and the Canvas App Previewer. If your canvas app will be shown in the navigation menu, we recommend that you use a 60x60 pixel size icon and let Salesforce automatically resize the icon to the smaller size that is needed for the Chatter tab and the Canvas App Previewer.

You can also customize the icon that is used in the Salesforce1 publisher for a canvas app. The publisher uses the custom icon set for the action that accesses the canvas app, not the custom icon that is associated with the connected app. See Custom Icon Guidelines and Best Practices on page 62 for more guidelines on custom action icons.

CHAPTER 17 Learning More

In addition to this guide, there are many resources available to help you in your Salesforce1 Platform development journey.

Admin Resources

Salesforce Help & Training Portal
A site devoted to the help documentation for Salesforce. Get help for what you're working on, find answers to your questions, and download tip sheets and other guides.

Salesforce Success Community
Home to a set of extremely useful tools to help you get your Salesforce work done. Connect with salesforce.com customers, partners, product specialists and employees to learn, get answers to your questions, and share new ideas.

Salesforce Developers Website

Our premier developer site is a one-stop shop for all things related to Salesforce1 Platform development. On Salesforce Developers you'll find documentation, code samples, tools, articles, discussion boards, and other resources to help you get started with mobile development.

Developer Documentation

You'll find all these guides and more on our developer site at
`http://developer.salesforce.com/docs`.

Publisher Actions Implementation Guide
Learn about the default actions, how to create object-specific actions, and how to configure publisher layouts. Find out how you can extend the publisher with Visualforce custom actions and Force.com Canvas custom actions.

Salesforce1 Platform API Services Guide
Learn about all the Salesforce1 Platform APIs and how to use them to integrate all your apps.

Mobile App Developer Guide

Learn about native iOS and Android, HTML5, and hybrid mobile development. This guide also includes information about more advanced topics such as authentication, geolocation, and distributing your mobile apps.

Force.com Canvas Developer's Guide

Learn about integrating Web applications with Salesforce1 using Force.com Canvas. You'll learn how to get up to speed quickly with quick starts, how to use the Force.com Canvas SDK, and about the context objects.

Chatter REST API Developer's Guide

Learn how to programmatically access Chatter feed and social data like users, groups, followers, and files. You'll learn how to get up to speed quickly with quick starts and how to call the various Chatter REST resources.

Force.com REST API Developer's Guide

Learn to use the REST-based API to retrieve, create, update, and delete data in Salesforce. You'll learn how to get up to speed quickly with quick starts, about the available REST API resources, and how to make calls and work with data.

Visualforce Developer's Guide

Learn how to use Visualforce to customize and extend the Salesforce user interface.

Force.com SOQL and SOSL Reference

Learn how to use SOQL and SOSL to build powerful queries and text searches.

INDEX

A

About Acme Wireless 12
About the sample scenario 12
About this book
    audience 12
    how do I begin? 12
Actions
    about action layouts 52
    about custom actions 59
    about predefined values 56
    assigning to a global page layout 51
    assigning to a page layout 50
    create actions 46
    creating 49
    creating a global action 51
    creating an object-specific action 49–50
    custom actions 47
    customizing an action layout 54
    default actions 47
    global actions 46
    guidelines and best practices 62
    log a call actions 46
    mobile smart actions 47
    object-specific actions 46, 49, 55
    overview for mobile 45
    predefined values for actions 58
    setting a predefined field value 57
    standard actions 47
    tell me more 52
    testing in Salesforce1 55, 58
    update actions 46
    what they are 46
Actions, calling from the API
    add the code to call the action 137
    create an action 136
    overview 135

Actions, calling from the API (continued)
    REST API resources 142
    test it out 139
Add the Visualforce tab to the navigation menu 82
Audience for Part II, developer guide 66

B

business scenario, Acme Wireless 66

C

Canvas apps in the feed
    about the code to create feed items 133
    add the action to the publisher layout 126
    clone the third-party Web application 119
    configure the Heroku environment variable 123
    configure who can access the canvas app 123
    create a global action 125
    create the canvas app 121
canvas apps in the feed introduction 119
Canvas custom actions
    add the action to the publisher layout 110
    clone the third-party Web application 105
    configure the Heroku environment variable 109
    configure who can access the canvas app 108
    create the canvas app 106
    get context in your canvas app 114
    introduction 104
    test canvas apps in the feed in Salesforce1 127
    test the canvas custom action in Salesforce1 111
canvas custom actions introduction 104
Compact layouts
    creating 40

Index

Compact layouts *(continued)*
    find out more 43
    overview 39
    overview for mobile 31
    test it out 42
    try it out 40
Configuring and enabling offline access 21
Configuring Salesforce1 17–18
Create a Visualforce page 78
Create a Visualforce tab 81
Custom actions
    add the Visualforce custom action to the page
        layout 93
    business scenario 92
    create a Visualforce custom action 92
    introduction 91
    test the Visualforce custom action in the
        Salesforce1 app 94
custom actions introduction 91

D

development process for Salesforce1 68

F

Flexible Pages
    about 162
    adding an action 160
    adding to Salesforce1 navigation menu 164
    assigning actions 159
    available components 154
    create a tab 162
    creating 156–158
    deploying 161
    downloading the sample app 157
    overview 153–154
    structure 154
    tell me more 163, 167
    test it out 165
Force.com Canvas
    best practices 205–206, 208–209

Force.com Canvas features 104
Force.com Canvas introduction 103

G

Guidelines and best practices
    actions 62
    custom icons 62
    for administrators 61
    for developers 169

I

Introduction 1

L

Learning more
    development resources 211

N

Navigation menu
    when to use 170
Notifications
    about 19
    approval requests 20
    enabling 20

O

overview of calling actions from the API 135

P

Page layouts
    creating a mobile-optimized layout 35
    how they work in Salesforce1 32
    optimizing for mobile 38
    overview for mobile 31
    rethinking for mobile 33
    test it out 36
Prerequisites for Salesforce1 development 69
Publisher
    when to use 170

S

Salesforce1
about 4
comparison to other mobile apps 9
configuring 17–18
configuring offline access 21
defining users 18
enabling offline access 21
notifications, about 19
notifications, approval requests 20
notifications, enabling 20
overview 9
what it looks like 5
Salesforce1 development
about the code to create feed items 133
about the Visualforce custom action code 97
about the Visualforce page code 87
best practices 169–174, 177, 183–184, 188,
191, 193, 196, 200, 203–206, 208–209
business scenario 66
canvas apps in the feed 119, 121, 123, 125–
127
canvas custom actions 104–106, 108–110
custom actions 91–94, 111
custom actions scenario 92
development process 68
Flexible Pages 164
Force.com Canvas 103, 169, 205
Force.com Canvas apps in the feed 208
Force.com Canvas apps in the publisher 206
Force.com Canvas context 208
Force.com Canvas custom icons 209
Force.com Canvas features 104
get Salesforce context 114
introduction 65
prerequisites 69
Visualforce 169, 171–174, 177, 183–184, 188,
191, 193, 196, 200, 203–205
Visualforce pages 77–78, 81–83

Salesforce1 development *(continued)*
where Visualforce pages can be accessed 85
who this part is for 66
Salesforce1 navigation menu
about 26
configuring 27
overview 25
tell me more 29
test it out 28
try it out 27
Salesforce1 Platform
features 2
overview 2
Salesforce1 Platform development
learning more 211
Salesforce1 Platform vs. custom apps 66
Setting up your work environment
downloading and configuring Salesforce1 16
importing warehouse data model 16
setting your default page layout 69

U

User interface guidelines
design for mobile 72
introduction 71
keep navigation simple 72
minimize the number of fields 73
minimize user interface text 74
put important information at the top 72
tap target size 75
use field defaults 74

V

Visualforce custom actions
about the custom action code 97
add the Visualforce custom action to the page
layout 93
create a Visualforce custom action 92
test the Visualforce custom action in the
Salesforce1 app 94

Index

Visualforce pages in the navigation menu
    about the controller and page code 87
    add the tab to the navigation menu 82
    create a page 78
    create a tab 81
    introduction 77
    test your page in the Salesforce1 app 83

Visualforce pages introduction 77

W

When to use the Mobile SDK 66
When to use the Salesforce1 Platform 66